Sedona Travel Guide 2025

Discover A Combination Of Natural Beauty, Outdoor Adventure And Spiritual Renewal From The Red Rocks of Cathedral Rock To Bell Rock

Lucas D. King

Lucas D. King

SEDONA

GALLERY

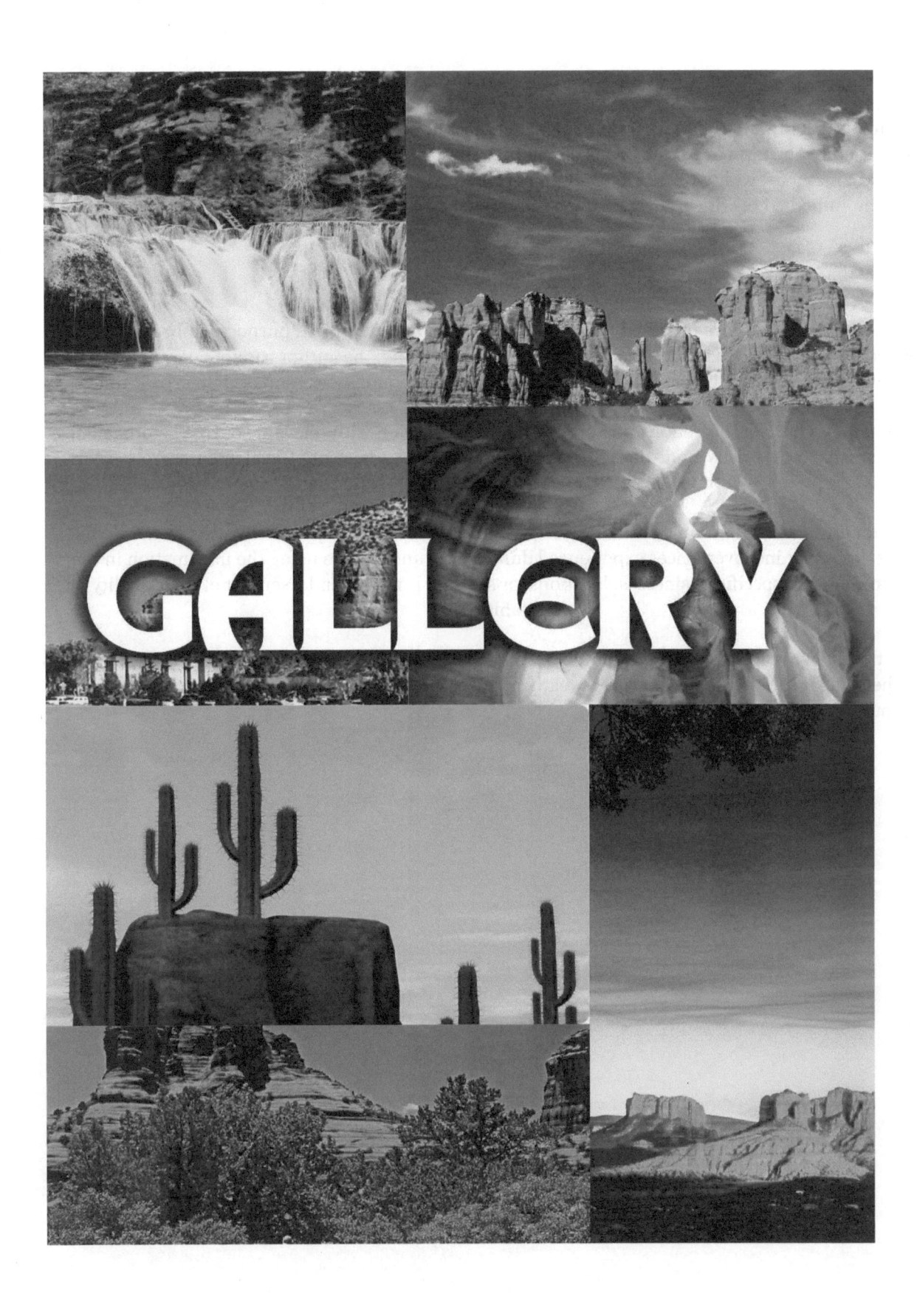

Copyright

2025 Lucas D. King. All rights reserved. No part of this publication may be reproduced, distributed, or transmitted in any form or by any means, including photocopying, recording, or other electronic or mechanical methods, without the prior written permission of the publisher, except in the case of brief quotations embodied in critical reviews and certain other noncommercial uses permitted by copyright law.

Disclaimer

The contents of this book are provided for informational and entertainment purposes only. While every effort has been made to ensure accuracy at the time of writing, the author cannot guarantee the completeness or reliability of all details, as attractions, costs, and services may change over time.

Readers should use their discretion and verify current information with relevant sources before making travel arrangements. This guide does not replace professional advice or official updates from local authorities, tourism boards, or businesses mentioned.

Travel inherently involves some level of risk. The author accepts no responsibility for any accidents, injuries, losses, or inconveniences experienced during trips undertaken using the information in this book. Inclusion of specific businesses, locations, or services is not an endorsement of their quality or suitability.

By using this book, readers agree to take full responsibility for their decisions and experiences. Always double-check details, especially concerning weather, safety conditions, and availability, before setting out on your journey.

Table of Content

Welcome Section..7
Chapter 1: Welcome to Sedona..7
   The Allure of Sedona – Red Rocks and Beyond......................................7
   Personal Reflections: My Journey to Sedona...9
   Why This Guide..10
Chapter 2: Introduction to Sedona..11
   A Brief History of Sedona..11
   Geographical Overview and Climate...12
   Why Sedona Is a Must-Visit Destination..13
Planning Your Trip...14
Chapter 3: When to Visit Sedona..14
   Seasons and Weather Patterns...14
   Best Times for Hiking, Festivals, and Photography...............................14
Chapter 4: Getting to Sedona..16
   By Air: Closest Airports...16
   By Car: Driving Directions and Scenic Routes..16
   Public Transport and Shuttle Services..17
Chapter 5: What to Pack..18
   Essential Gear for Every Season..18
   Clothing Tips for Activities and Weather...18
Where to Stay...20
Chapter 6: Where to Stay...20
   Top Picks for Indulgence..20
   Mid-Range Hotels and Inns...21
   Motels, Hostels, and Camping Spots...23
   Vacation Rentals and Unique Lodgings..25
Exploring Sedona..27
Chapter 7: Iconic Landmarks and Natural Wonders..................................27
   Cathedral Rock...27
   Devil's Bridge...28
   Bell Rock..29
   Oak Creek Canyon and Slide Rock State Park..31
   Red Rock Crossing and Crescent Moon Picnic Site...............................33
Chapter 8: Sedona's Vortex Sites..35
   What Are Vortexes?..35
   A Guide to Spiritual and Energetic Experiences.....................................35
Chapter 9: Best Hiking Trails in Sedona...37
   A Guide to Spiritual and Energetic Experiences.....................................37
Chapter 10: Outdoor Adventures in Sedona..41
   Jeep Tours, Hot Air Balloon Rides, and Mountain Biking....................41
Chapter 11: Sedona's Art Scene..43
   Must-Visit Galleries and Studios...43
Chapter 12: Historical and Cultural Landmarks..45

    Chapel of the Holy Cross, Palatki Heritage Site, and More..45
    Historical Significance and Visitor Information..46
Chapter 13: Festivals and Events in Sedona.. 49
    Art Fairs, Music Festivals, and Cultural Celebrations..49
Culinary Adventures... 51
Chapter 14: Local Cuisine and Dining Scene... 51
    Top Restaurants and Cafes.. 51
    Regional Dishes You Can't Miss..52
Chapter 15: Farm-to-Table and Organic Dining..55
    Supporting Local Farmers and Sustainable Practices..55
    Food Tours and Unique Experiences... 55
Practical Guide..57
Chapter 16: Sustainable and Responsible Travel..57
    Tips for Minimizing Your Environmental Impact..57
    How to Respect Sedona's Culture and Environment...57
Chapter 17: Safety and Etiquette.. 59
    Trail Safety and Emergency Contacts.. 59
    Local Customs and Dos and Don'ts.. 59
Chapter 18: Planning Resources..61
    Sample Itineraries..61
    Sedona for Families...63
    Sedona for Couples...66
    Sedona for Solo Travelers... 69
Chapter 19: Frequently Asked Questions (FAQs)..72
    Common Concerns Addressed... 72
Additional Resources..74
    Websites, Apps, and Local Contacts... 74
Bonus...75
    Budget Plans.. 75
    3- Day Travel Journal... 77

Welcome Section

Chapter 1: Welcome to Sedona

The Allure of Sedona – Red Rocks and Beyond

As you approach Sedona, whether winding through Oak Creek Canyon or cresting the hills from the Verde Valley, the landscape transforms before your eyes. Towering red rock formations, with their bold, fiery hues, rise dramatically against the backdrop of an endless blue sky. There's something almost magical about the way the sun plays with the sandstone, casting shifting shadows that make the scenery look alive. Sedona doesn't just greet you; it draws you in, promising adventure, serenity, and a deep connection to nature.

The allure of Sedona lies not just in its breathtaking scenery but in the energy that seems to emanate from the land itself. It's no wonder that Sedona is often called the "most beautiful place on Earth." The rock formations have names that evoke their grandeur and mystique—Cathedral Rock, Bell Rock, Courthouse Butte—and each carries a unique story, whether geological, spiritual, or cultural. Visitors from around the globe come not only to marvel at these natural wonders but to feel their presence, as if the land is alive with stories of its ancient past.

Sedona's magic extends beyond the red rocks. The vibrant energy of the area is said to center around its famous vortexes—locations where the earth's energy is believed to be especially strong. Whether you buy into the mysticism or simply feel reinvigorated by the incredible vistas, there's no denying that Sedona has a way of grounding and inspiring everyone who visits. Artists find their muse in the shifting colors of the cliffs; hikers find solace on trails that wind through rugged terrain; and spiritual seekers come looking for clarity under the wide desert sky.

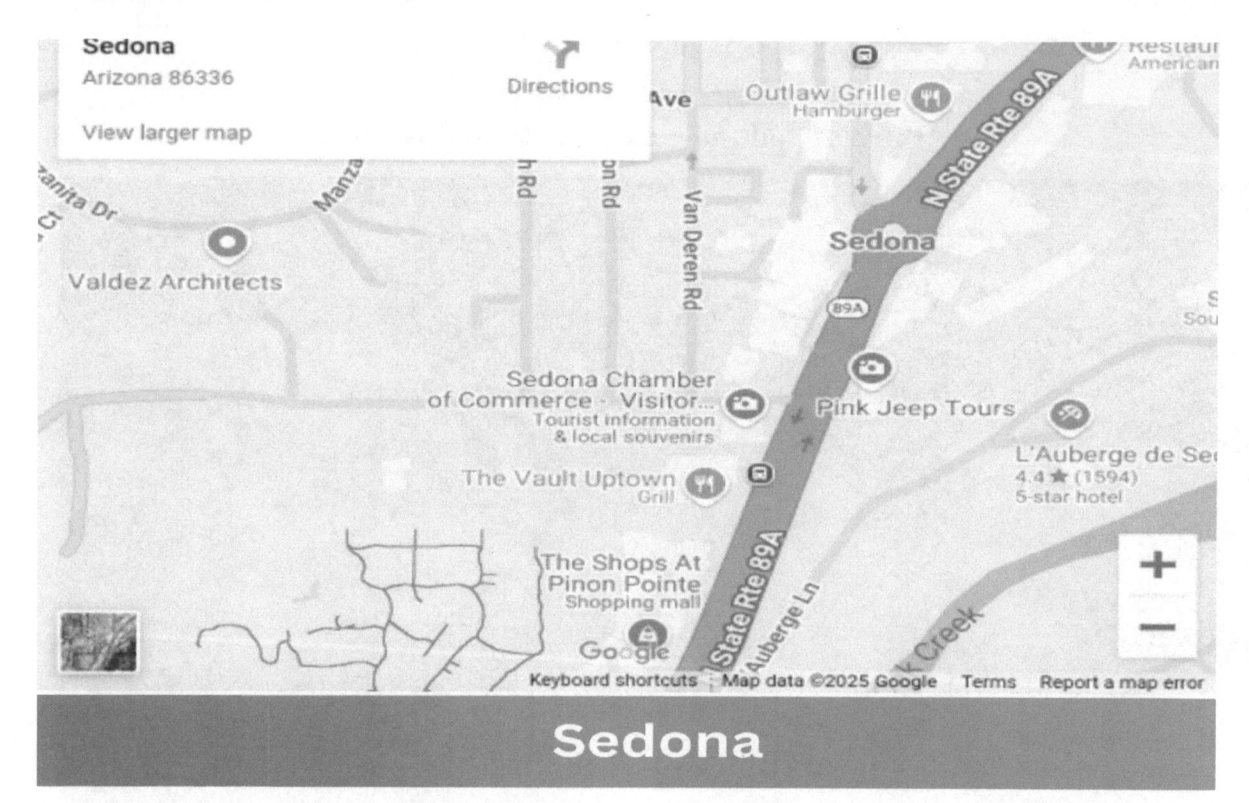

SCAN THE QR CODE

1. Open your device's camera app.
2. Point the camera at the QR code.
3. Hold steady and wait for recognition.
4. Review the displayed information.
5. Follow the prompt to access the content.

Yet Sedona is more than its natural wonders. It's a place where luxury meets ruggedness, where fine dining and boutique shopping coexist with hiking boots and dusty trails. Visitors can wake up to the soft glow of sunrise over the red rocks, spend the day exploring hidden canyons or enjoying a jeep tour, and end the evening with a glass of local wine under a canopy of stars.

Sedona invites you to look beyond its iconic landscapes and immerse yourself in the experiences it offers. Whether you're here to hike, meditate, paint, or simply soak in the beauty, Sedona is a place where memories are made, and where you can't help but leave a piece of your heart behind. It's not just a destination—it's a journey into the extraordinary.

Personal Reflections: My Journey to Sedona

Sedona first appeared in my life like an unassuming gift, one that slowly revealed its treasures the more time I spent with it. The first time I visited, I was a wide-eyed traveler, eager to see the famed red rocks I had heard so much about. I'll never forget my first glimpse of Cathedral Rock—it was like walking into a painting. The air felt cleaner, the colors sharper, and the silence... oh, the silence was a presence all its own. I spent that trip hiking trails with no clear plan, just letting Sedona lead me. It was a fleeting but powerful introduction to the magic of this place.

Years later, Sedona came back into my life, not as a brief escape, but as a home. I lived there during a transformative chapter of my life, and those red rocks became more than just a backdrop; they became companions. I learned their moods—how the light dances across the formations at sunrise, how they seem to glow with an inner fire at sunset, and how they fade into deep purples under a blanket of stars. Living in Sedona allowed me to slow down and really listen to what the land had to say. It wasn't just a destination anymore; it became a sanctuary.

Returning to Sedona later, after some years away, felt like a reunion with an old friend. I noticed things I hadn't before—the way the juniper trees twist and tangle, as if trying to reach the sky, and the sweet, herbal scent of sage that seems to linger in the air. The vortexes, which I had once dismissed as mere myth, began to make sense to me in ways that are hard to put into words. It wasn't just the beauty of the place but the energy of it. Sedona is a land that invites introspection, where the quiet moments seem to hold answers you didn't know you were looking for.

Through my many encounters with Sedona—whether as a first-time visitor, a temporary resident, or a returning traveler—I've come to appreciate it in layers. It's not just the landscapes, though they are breathtaking. It's the people, too—the artists who find endless inspiration here, the locals who know secret trails and hidden swimming holes, and even the fellow travelers who come seeking something they can't quite name. It's the rhythm of Sedona that captivates you, the way it beckons you to slow down and pay attention.

This guide is born from those experiences—moments of discovery, stillness, and wonder that I hope you'll find for yourself. Sedona has given me so much, and I'm thrilled to share its secrets, stories, and spirit with you. Whether you're coming for the first time or the tenth, I promise there's always something new to discover here. Let's explore Sedona together, one breathtaking view at a time.

Why This Guide

When planning a trip to a place as remarkable as Sedona, it's easy to get overwhelmed by the sheer abundance of choices. Do you hike to the iconic Devil's Bridge or explore a less-traveled trail that winds through a quiet canyon? Should you indulge in a luxurious spa day or dive headfirst into a rugged outdoor adventure? Where do you find the best sunset views or a meal that feels as inspired as the scenery? These are the questions I've faced during my own visits to Sedona—and the reason this guide exists.

This isn't just another travel guide filled with generic recommendations and surface-level information. It's a curated companion born out of years of experience—both as a first-time visitor discovering Sedona's highlights and as someone who has lived here, immersed in its daily rhythms. I've been that traveler marveling at the grandeur of Cathedral Rock for the first time, and I've been the local uncovering hidden gems you won't find on most tourist maps.

In this guide, you'll find more than just lists of attractions or places to stay. You'll get thoughtful insights on what makes each experience special and practical advice to help you make the most of your time. From the top-rated hiking trails to serene spots only the locals know, I've poured everything I've learned into these pages. Whether you're looking for the perfect itinerary, an unforgettable dining experience, or tips to connect with Sedona's unique energy, this guide has you covered.

But what truly sets this guide apart is the perspective it brings. It combines the awe of a visitor with the familiarity of a local. You'll find inspiration for adventure, detailed advice to avoid the pitfalls of planning, and reflections that go deeper than the usual tourist takeaways.

Sedona is more than a destination; it's an experience, a feeling, a memory waiting to be made. My hope is that this guide helps you discover the Sedona that speaks to you—a Sedona that surprises, captivates, and stays with you long after you leave. Let this guide be your trusted companion as you begin your journey to one of the most beautiful and inspiring places in the world.

Chapter 2: Introduction to Sedona

A Brief History of Sedona

Sedona's history is as rich and layered as the red rocks that define its skyline. To truly appreciate this remarkable place, it helps to look beyond its striking natural beauty and delve into the stories of the people and events that have shaped it over millennia. Sedona is not just a scenic destination; it is a living tapestry of ancient cultures, pioneering spirit, and a modern-day commitment to preserving its unique character.

Long before Sedona became a hub for artists, adventurers, and spiritual seekers, it was home to the Native American tribes who first inhabited this land. The area is part of the ancestral homelands of the Sinagua people, who lived here from around 600 to 1400 CE. Evidence of their presence can still be found in the remarkable ruins of cliff dwellings, such as those at Montezuma Castle and Tuzigoot, as well as in the intricate petroglyphs and pictographs that adorn the rocks in places like the Palatki and Honanki Heritage Sites. These ancient peoples cultivated the land, growing corn, beans, and squash, and developed an intimate relationship with the environment that is reflected in their art and architecture.

Following the mysterious departure of the Sinagua, the Yavapai and Apache tribes made the region their home. For these tribes, the red rocks held deep spiritual significance, and the land provided sustenance and a profound connection to their cultural heritage. Tragically, their way of life was disrupted in the 19th century with the arrival of European settlers, who brought ranching, farming, and eventually the railroad.

The late 19th century saw Sedona begin its transformation into the community we know today. Homesteaders like T.C. Schnebly arrived in the area, drawn by its fertile land and stunning surroundings. Schnebly, for whom the town is named, is often credited with putting Sedona on the map. He built a post office and submitted his wife Sedona's name for the town—a choice that gives Sedona a personal, human touch even in its official history.

By the early 20th century, Sedona's charm caught the attention of Hollywood. The towering red rock formations served as the perfect backdrop for Westerns, and the town quickly became known as "Arizona's Little Hollywood." Some films brought Sedona to audiences around the world, further enhancing its mystique and allure.

In more recent decades, Sedona has become synonymous with artistic creativity, wellness, and spirituality. The discovery and promotion of Sedona's vortex sites in the 1980s positioned the town as a center for healing and meditation, drawing seekers and practitioners from all corners of the globe. Meanwhile, the burgeoning art scene, supported by galleries and festivals, solidified Sedona's reputation as a haven for creative minds.

Today, Sedona continues to honor its past while embracing its future. It is a place where ancient petroglyphs coexist with world-class resorts, where hiking trails reveal the echoes of history, and where the timeless beauty of the landscape serves as a reminder of the enduring power of nature and culture. This brief history is just the beginning—Sedona's story is still being written, and each visitor who experiences its wonders becomes a part of that legacy.

Geographical Overview and Climate

Sedona is nestled in the heart of northern Arizona, where the Colorado Plateau, the Mogollon Rim, and the Verde Valley converge to create one of the most geologically stunning landscapes in the world. Located approximately 120 miles north of Phoenix and 30 miles south of Flagstaff, Sedona sits at an elevation of about 4,350 feet. This high-desert region is characterized by its iconic red rock formations, lush riparian zones, and an array of ecosystems that support diverse plant and animal life.

The red rocks for which Sedona is famous owe their color to a high concentration of iron oxide in the sandstone layers. These formations are part of the Schnebly Hill Formation, which dates back over 275 million years to an ancient inland sea. Erosion, time, and tectonic activity have sculpted these breathtaking formations into buttes, spires, and mesas that captivate geologists and visitors alike.

Sedona's geography is further enhanced by the presence of Oak Creek, a tributary of the Verde River. The creek carves a green oasis through the arid landscape, supporting cottonwoods, sycamores, and willows that contrast vividly with the red rocks. This unique combination of desert and riparian zones creates a rare biodiversity, making Sedona a haven for wildlife enthusiasts and nature lovers.

The climate in Sedona is classified as semi-arid, with mild winters and warm summers. Winter temperatures average between 30°F and 60°F, while summer highs typically range from 80°F to 100°F. The area enjoys over 300 days of sunshine annually, making it a year-round destination. However, the summer monsoon season (July to September) brings dramatic thunderstorms, adding to the allure of Sedona's ever-changing landscape.

Why Sedona Is a Must-Visit Destination

Sedona is more than a picturesque location; it is a multifaceted destination that appeals to adventurers, artists, and seekers of tranquility alike. Its combination of natural beauty, unique cultural offerings, and recreational opportunities makes it one of the most extraordinary places to visit in the United States.

1. Stunning Natural Landscapes
Sedona's red rock formations are among the most photographed natural wonders in the world. Iconic landmarks such as Cathedral Rock, Bell Rock, and Courthouse Butte draw millions of visitors each year. These formations are not just visually stunning but also accessible, with trails for every skill level leading to breathtaking views and serene canyons.

2. Outdoor Recreation
The area boasts over 200 miles of hiking and biking trails, ranging from easy strolls like the Bell Rock Pathway to challenging climbs like Bear Mountain. Jeep tours, hot air balloon rides, and horseback riding are popular ways to explore Sedona's rugged terrain. For those seeking water-based activities, Oak Creek offers excellent opportunities for fishing, swimming, and picnicking.

3. Cultural and Artistic Heritage
Sedona has a thriving arts scene, with over 80 galleries showcasing everything from traditional Native American crafts to contemporary sculpture and painting. The annual Sedona International Film Festival and Sedona Arts Festival attract artists and audiences from around the globe. The town's vibrant cultural offerings complement its natural wonders, providing a well-rounded visitor experience.

4. Wellness and Spiritual Appeal
Sedona is renowned for its vortex sites, areas believed to radiate concentrated earth energy. These locations—such as Bell Rock, Cathedral Rock, and Airport Mesa—draw spiritual seekers and practitioners of alternative healing. The town is also home to numerous spas, wellness retreats, and yoga centers, making it a haven for relaxation and rejuvenation.

5. Accessibility and Amenities
Despite its remote feel, Sedona is easily accessible via major highways and is well-equipped with accommodations ranging from luxury resorts to charming bed-and-breakfasts. Its culinary scene is equally impressive, offering everything from fine dining to casual eateries that highlight regional flavors and locally sourced ingredients.

6. Year-Round Appeal
Sedona's mild climate makes it a year-round destination. Spring wildflowers, autumn foliage, and the occasional winter snowfall add seasonal beauty, while events like the Sedona Mountain Bike Festival and Hummingbird Festival ensure there is always something to do.

Sedona is a must-visit destination because it offers an unparalleled combination of natural beauty, outdoor adventure, cultural enrichment, and spiritual renewal. Whether you're seeking a challenging hike, artistic inspiration, or a peaceful retreat, Sedona has something to offer every kind of traveler.

Planning Your Trip

Chapter 3: When to Visit Sedona

Sedona is a year-round destination, but the best time to visit depends on your interests and tolerance for crowds and weather. Here's a breakdown of seasons and what they offer:

Seasons and Weather Patterns

Spring (March to May)

- **Weather:** Temperatures range from 45°F to 75°F, with cooler mornings and evenings. Wildflowers bloom, adding vibrant colors to the landscape.
- **Crowds:** One of the busiest times, so book accommodations and tours in advance.
- **Key Features:** Ideal for outdoor activities, as the weather is mild and pleasant.

Summer (June to August)

- **Weather:** Highs range from 80°F to 100°F. Afternoons often bring monsoon thunderstorms, providing dramatic skies and cooler evenings.
- **Crowds:** Moderate, with fewer visitors compared to spring and fall.
- **Key Features:** Oak Creek provides a cool retreat with swimming and picnicking opportunities. Morning hikes are best to avoid midday heat.

Fall (September to November)

- **Weather:** Temperatures range from 45°F to 75°F, similar to spring but with less fluctuation. Fall foliage adds golden hues to the already stunning scenery.
- **Crowds:** Another peak season, especially in October and November.
- **Key Features:** Excellent for hiking and photography due to cooler weather and vibrant landscapes.

Winter (December to February)

- **Weather:** Daytime highs average 50°F to 60°F, with colder mornings and occasional snow dusting the red rocks.
- **Crowds:** Lowest of the year, making it ideal for a quieter visit.
- **Key Features:** Perfect for those seeking solitude, discounted lodging rates, and a serene atmosphere.

Best Times for Hiking, Festivals, and Photography

Hiking

- **Best Seasons:** Spring and fall offer optimal temperatures for long hikes like West Fork Trail and Cathedral Rock.
- **Winter Tips:** Trails are less crowded, but icy conditions can occur on shaded paths.
- **Summer Advice:** Stick to early morning or evening hikes to avoid extreme heat.

Festivals

- **Spring:** The Sedona Yoga Festival (March) and Sedona International Film Festival (February/March) attract large crowds and diverse activities.
- **Fall:** The Sedona Arts Festival (October) and Dia de los Muertos Celebration (November) highlight the region's cultural vibrancy.

Photography

- **Best Times:** Sunrise and sunset year-round provide the best lighting for capturing the red rocks.
- **Seasonal Highlights:** Spring wildflowers, summer monsoon clouds, fall foliage, and winter snow each add unique elements to photographs.

In summary, spring and fall are the most popular seasons for their mild weather and vibrant landscapes, while winter and summer cater to those seeking fewer crowds and unique seasonal experiences. Plan your visit based on your priorities to make the most of Sedona's unparalleled beauty and activities.

Chapter 4: Getting to Sedona

Sedona is a relatively remote destination, but its accessibility is enhanced by nearby airports, well-maintained highways, and shuttle services. Understanding the transportation options will help you plan a smooth and enjoyable journey.

By Air: Closest Airports

1. **Phoenix Sky Harbor International Airport (PHX)**

   - **Distance:** Approximately 120 miles (2 hours by car).
   - **Overview:** The largest and most popular gateway to Sedona, offering flights from most major cities worldwide.
   - **Transport Options:** Rental cars, shuttle services (such as Groome Transportation), and rideshares are readily available.

2. **Flagstaff Pulliam Airport (FLG)**

   - **Distance:** About 30 miles (45 minutes by car).
   - **Overview:** A smaller regional airport with limited flights, primarily from Phoenix.
   - **Transport Options:** Rental cars and limited shuttle services to Sedona.

3. **Prescott Regional Airport (PRC)**

   - **Distance:** Approximately 65 miles (1.5 hours by car).
   - **Overview:** Another regional airport with limited domestic flights, primarily serving nearby cities in Arizona.
   - **Transport Options:** Rental cars are available, but shuttle services may require prior arrangements.

By Car: Driving Directions and Scenic Routes

Sedona is most easily accessed by car, which also allows you to enjoy the stunning scenery along the way.

1. **From Phoenix (via I-17 and AZ-179)**

   - **Distance:** 120 miles (2 hours).
   - **Route Highlights:** The journey takes you north on I-17, followed by a turn onto AZ-179, designated as the "Red Rock Scenic Byway." This stretch offers breathtaking views of Sedona's red rocks as you approach.

2. **From Flagstaff (via AZ-89A)**

   - **Distance:** 30 miles (45 minutes).
   - **Route Highlights:** The drive south on AZ-89A winds through Oak Creek Canyon, known for its lush forest, dramatic cliffs, and spectacular switchbacks.

3. **From Las Vegas (via US-93, I-40, and AZ-89A)**

   - **Distance:** 280 miles (4.5 hours).
   - **Route Highlights:** A longer but scenic route that passes through the Mojave Desert and the Kaibab National Forest before descending into Sedona's red rock country.

4. **From Albuquerque (via I-40 and AZ-89A)**
   - **Distance:** 380 miles (6 hours).
   - **Route Highlights:** This route takes you through historic Route 66 towns and the stunning landscapes of northern Arizona.

Public Transport and Shuttle Services

Sedona has limited public transportation, but several shuttle services and tour operators help visitors navigate the region.

1. **Groome Transportation**

   - **Route:** Operates daily shuttles between Phoenix Sky Harbor International Airport and Sedona.
   - **Cost:** $68 per adult one-way; discounts for children and seniors.
   - **Details:** The shuttle drops passengers at central locations in Sedona, with prior bookings required.

2. **Sedona Trolley**

   - **Route:** Operates within Sedona, offering tours and hop-on-hop-off services to key attractions.
   - **Cost:** $15 for a one-hour tour; free for children under 5.
   - **Details:** Covers popular destinations like Tlaquepaque Arts Village, Uptown Sedona, and Chapel of the Holy Cross.

3. **Cottonwood Area Transit (CAT)**

   - **Route:** Limited service between Cottonwood, Verde Valley, and Sedona.
   - **Cost:** $1 per ride; $2 for a day pass.
   - **Details:** This is the most affordable option but has infrequent schedules.

4. **Private Shuttle Services**

   - **Examples:** Sedona-Phoenix Shuttle, Red Rock Transportation.
   - **Cost:** $50–$80 per person, depending on distance and service type.
   - **Details:** Offers door-to-door service for groups or individuals.

Driving remains the most convenient way to get to and around Sedona, especially for those wanting to explore the surrounding areas. However, shuttles from Phoenix and Flagstaff provide hassle-free options for those who prefer not to drive. Plan ahead, particularly during peak seasons, to ensure your transportation aligns with your itinerary.

Chapter 5: What to Pack

Proper preparation ensures a comfortable and enjoyable experience in Sedona, no matter the season or planned activities. Here's a direct guide to essential gear and clothing tips tailored to Sedona's climate and outdoor adventures.

Essential Gear for Every Season

1. **Reusable Water Bottles or Hydration Packs:** Staying hydrated is crucial in Sedona's dry climate. Carry at least 2 liters per person, especially for hikes.
2. **Daypack:** A lightweight, durable backpack for carrying water, snacks, sunscreen, and other essentials.
3. **Sunscreen and Lip Balm:** Protect your skin from the high-altitude sun. Choose SPF 30 or higher.
4. **Hat and Sunglasses:** Wide-brim hats and UV-protective sunglasses are essential for sun protection.
5. **Sturdy Hiking Shoes or Boots:** Opt for shoes with good traction to navigate rocky trails and uneven terrain.
6. **Map or GPS Device:** Cell service can be spotty on trails, so carry a physical map or a reliable GPS device.
7. **First Aid Kit:** Include band-aids, antiseptic wipes, and blister treatments.
8. **Snacks and Energy Bars:** Pack non-perishable, high-energy snacks for hikes and day trips.
9. **Flashlight or Headlamp:** Essential for early-morning or late-evening hikes.

Clothing Tips for Activities and Weather

Spring (March to May)

- **Clothing:** Lightweight layers, long-sleeved shirts for sun protection, and a windbreaker for breezy mornings and evenings.
- **Shoes:** Comfortable hiking boots for daytime activities and casual shoes for exploring town.

Summer (June to August)

- **Clothing:** Breathable, moisture-wicking fabrics, shorts, and sleeveless tops for hot days. A lightweight rain jacket is useful during afternoon monsoons.
- **Shoes:** Sandals or water shoes for creek activities, in addition to sturdy hiking footwear.

Fall (September to November)

- **Clothing:** Layers are key—pack short-sleeved shirts for daytime and warmer jackets or sweaters for cooler evenings.
- **Shoes:** Durable hiking shoes for trail exploration and comfortable shoes for casual outings.

Winter (December to February)

- **Clothing:** Insulated jackets, thermal layers, gloves, and a hat for chilly mornings and evenings. Fleece or down vests work well during the day.
- **Shoes:** Waterproof hiking boots are recommended, as trails may be icy or muddy.

Activity-Specific Recommendations

- **Hiking:** Moisture-wicking socks, hiking poles, and gaiters for dusty trails.
- **Photography:** Gloves with touchscreen tips for winter shoots, a lens cleaner, and protective gear for cameras.
- **Festivals and Events:** Casual but presentable clothing, comfortable walking shoes, and a light jacket for cooler evenings.
- **Creekside Activities:** Swimwear, quick-drying towels, and water shoes.

By tailoring your packing list to the season and your planned activities, you'll be ready to fully enjoy everything Sedona has to offer.

Where to Stay

Chapter 6: Where to Stay

Top Picks for Indulgence

Sedona offers some of the most opulent and serene accommodations, perfect for travelers looking to indulge in the natural beauty of the red rocks while enjoying world-class amenities. Here are six top luxury resorts and spas, along with their features, costs, and booking tips.

1. Enchantment Resort

- **Overview:** Nestled in the heart of Boynton Canyon, this resort combines luxury with breathtaking views of Sedona's iconic red rock formations. Each casita offers a blend of Southwestern charm and modern comfort.
- **Why Go:** The resort is a haven for those seeking relaxation, adventure, and cultural immersion. It boasts access to exclusive hiking trails, a top-tier spa, and Native American-inspired activities.
- **Amenities:** Mii amo Spa, multiple pools, on-site fine dining at Che Ah Chi, and outdoor activities like stargazing and yoga.
- **Cost:** Rooms start at $700 per night, with suites and casitas going upwards of $1,500 per night.
- **Booking Tips:** Book directly through the resort's website for special packages that include spa treatments or dining credits.

2. L'Auberge de Sedona

- **Overview:** Located along Oak Creek, this luxurious retreat offers a tranquil setting with individual cottages, creekside dining, and personalized service.
- **Why Go:** The resort provides an intimate connection to nature without sacrificing luxury. It's perfect for couples and those seeking a romantic getaway.
- **Amenities:** Creekside massages, outdoor soaking tubs, private balconies, and fine dining at Cress on Oak Creek.
- **Cost:** Rates start at $600 per night, with premium creekside cottages priced at $1,200–$1,800 per night.
- **Booking Tips:** Reserve during weekdays for better rates, and inquire about seasonal promotions that include breakfast or spa services.

3. Amara Resort and Spa

- **Overview:** Tucked within Uptown Sedona, this boutique resort combines contemporary design with a serene ambiance. Guests can enjoy stunning views of Snoopy Rock while lounging by the infinity pool.
- **Why Go:** Its central location is perfect for those who want to explore Sedona's shops and galleries while having a relaxing base to return to.
- **Amenities:** Saltwater infinity pool, complimentary yoga classes, pet-friendly accommodations, and the award-winning SaltRock Southwest Kitchen.
- **Cost:** Rates start at $450 per night.
- **Booking Tips:** Look for packages that combine dining or spa credits, particularly during shoulder seasons.

4. Adobe Grand Villas

- **Overview:** A unique boutique property offering individually themed villas with luxurious amenities and personalized touches, such as in-room fresh-baked bread.
- **Why Go:** This resort is perfect for travelers seeking a whimsical yet luxurious stay. Each villa feels like a private retreat, complete with hand-crafted details.
- **Amenities:** Private hot tubs, fireplaces, in-room dining options, and a gourmet breakfast included in the stay.
- **Cost:** Villas range from $550 to $900 per night.
- **Booking Tips:** Book well in advance, as this property is small and fills up quickly, especially during peak seasons.

5. Sedona Rouge Resort and Spa

- **Overview:** With a blend of Mediterranean-inspired architecture and modern luxury, this resort offers a sophisticated experience in West Sedona.
- **Why Go:** It's a great choice for travelers who want a quieter location with easy access to hiking trails and Sedona's main attractions.
- **Amenities:** A rooftop terrace with panoramic views, spa treatments featuring locally inspired therapies, and on-site dining at REDS Restaurant.
- **Cost:** Rooms start at $350 per night, with suites available for $600 and up.
- **Booking Tips:** Check for midweek deals, which often include complimentary spa services or dining discounts.

6. Mii amo (Wellness Destination at Enchantment)

- **Overview:** This world-renowned wellness retreat, located within the Enchantment Resort, offers an all-inclusive experience focused on holistic healing and rejuvenation.
- **Why Go:** Ideal for those looking for a transformative getaway. Guests can immerse themselves in tailored wellness programs, spa treatments, and healthy gourmet meals.
- **Amenities:** Private consultation sessions, guided meditation, fitness classes, and access to the Enchantment Resort facilities.
- **Cost:** Packages start at $1,500 per night per person, including accommodations, meals, and wellness activities.
- **Booking Tips:** Reservations are often required months in advance. Consider shoulder seasons for better availability and discounted rates.

Each of these resorts offers a unique blend of luxury, nature, and personalized service. Whether you're looking for creekside serenity, wellness-focused indulgence, or access to Sedona's vibrant culture, these options provide an unforgettable experience. Plan early, especially during peak seasons, to secure your stay at these sought-after properties.

Mid-Range Hotels and Inns

Sedona offers a range of mid-tier accommodations perfect for travelers seeking comfort, convenience, and affordability without sacrificing quality. Here are six excellent mid-range hotels and inns, with details on their highlights, locations, pricing, and reasons to choose them.

1. Sedona Real Inn and Suites

- **Overview:** A family-friendly hotel located in West Sedona, Sedona Real offers spacious suites and personalized service. The property is conveniently close to trails and attractions while maintaining a peaceful ambiance.
- **Why Go:** This inn strikes the perfect balance between cost and comfort, with complimentary breakfast and a dedicated concierge to help you plan activities. The large suites are ideal for families or groups.
- **Amenities:** Free hot breakfast, outdoor pool, pet-friendly accommodations, and a picnic area with barbecue grills.
- **Cost:** Rooms start at $180 per night, with suites priced at around $250.
- **Booking Tips:** Book directly for packages that include discounts on jeep tours or hiking guides.

2. The Andante Inn of Sedona

- **Overview:** Located near the base of Thunder Mountain, this hotel offers incredible views at an affordable price. Its central location makes it a convenient base for exploring Sedona's key attractions.
- **Why Go:** It's a practical choice for travelers who want scenic surroundings without splurging on luxury accommodations. The friendly staff and clean rooms make for a pleasant stay.
- **Amenities:** Free parking, seasonal outdoor pool, complimentary breakfast, and pet-friendly options.
- **Cost:** Rates typically range from $130 to $200 per night.
- **Booking Tips:** Look for discounts during off-peak months, especially in the winter.

3. Arroyo Pinion Hotel, Ascend Hotel Collection

- **Overview:** This boutique hotel offers a cozy and welcoming atmosphere, with Southwest-inspired décor and thoughtful amenities. It's located near West Sedona's shopping and dining districts.
- **Why Go:** Guests appreciate the clean, well-maintained rooms and the proximity to popular trails like the Airport Mesa Loop. It's also a good value for couples seeking a romantic getaway on a budget.
- **Amenities:** Outdoor hot tub, complimentary breakfast, in-room microwaves and fridges, and free Wi-Fi.
- **Cost:** Rooms start at $150 per night, with upgraded suites priced at $220.
- **Booking Tips:** Sign up for Choice Privileges for potential discounts or added perks.

4. Southwest Inn at Sedona

- **Overview:** A charming Southwestern-style inn known for its warm hospitality and comfortable accommodations. Its quiet location provides a relaxing retreat after a day of exploring.
- **Why Go:** The adobe-style architecture and mountain views give this in a distinctly Sedona feel. It's a perfect option for travelers who want a peaceful stay without venturing too far from the action.
- **Amenities:** Outdoor pool, hot tub, fireplaces in select rooms, and complimentary breakfast.
- **Cost:** Rooms range from $160 to $230 per night.
- **Booking Tips:** Request a room with a fireplace for added coziness during cooler months.

5. Bell Rock Inn by Diamond Resorts

- **Overview:** Situated near the iconic Bell Rock in the Village of Oak Creek, this property offers spacious rooms and suites with kitchenettes, making it an excellent choice for longer stays.
- **Why Go:** The location near Bell Rock and Courthouse Butte is perfect for outdoor enthusiasts. Plus, the kitchenette facilities allow you to save on dining expenses.
- **Amenities:** Outdoor pool, fitness center, BBQ facilities, and kitchenette-equipped rooms.
- **Cost:** Rates start at $140 per night for standard rooms, with suites priced at $200–$250.
- **Booking Tips:** Use Diamond Resorts' loyalty program for potential upgrades or discounted stays.

6. Sedona Village Lodge

- **Overview:** A no-frills yet comfortable lodge located in the Village of Oak Creek, offering incredible views of the red rocks at a wallet-friendly price.
- **Why Go:** If you're looking for affordability and convenience, this lodge is an excellent choice. It's near top attractions like Bell Rock and Cathedral Rock, making it a great base for hikers.
- **Amenities:** Free Wi-Fi, kitchenette options, and easy parking. Some rooms offer private balconies with views of the red rocks.
- **Cost:** Rates typically range from $110 to $180 per night.
- **Booking Tips:** Book a balcony room to enjoy stunning sunsets over the red rocks.

These mid-range options provide a great balance between cost and comfort, making them ideal for travelers who want to experience Sedona's beauty without overspending. Each property offers unique features that cater to different travel needs, from family-friendly amenities to romantic settings and convenient locations.

Motels, Hostels, and Camping Spots

For travelers on a tight budget, Sedona offers a variety of budget-friendly options including motels, hostels, and camping spots that provide comfortable stays and easy access to local attractions. Here's a list of affordable accommodations along with their features, costs, and reasons why you might consider them.

1. The Desert Quail Inn

- **Overview:** A no-frills motel located in Uptown Sedona, offering simple, clean rooms at a budget-friendly price.
- **Why Go:** It's an excellent choice for budget-conscious travelers who want to stay right in the heart of Sedona's shopping and dining district.
- **Amenities:** Free Wi-Fi, complimentary parking, and a seasonal outdoor pool.
- **Cost:** Rooms start at $90 per night.
- **Booking Tips:** Book early, as this inn fills up quickly during peak seasons.

2. Sedona International Hostel

- **Overview:** Located in a serene setting, this hostel offers a communal atmosphere ideal for solo travelers or backpackers.
- **Why Go:** It's a great option for budget travelers seeking a social environment, complete with shared dormitories and private rooms.
- **Amenities:** Free breakfast, Wi-Fi, shared kitchens, and common areas for socializing.
- **Cost:** Dormitory beds start at $30 per night, while private rooms are around $100.

- **Booking Tips:** Book in advance, especially if traveling during peak times like spring and fall.

3. Sedona RV & Camping Resort

- **Overview:** For those traveling in an RV or looking to camp, this resort offers spacious sites with full hookups and tent camping areas.
- **Why Go:** It's perfect for outdoor enthusiasts who want to stay close to nature and enjoy Sedona's scenic landscapes.
- **Amenities:** Full RV hookups, restrooms and showers, laundry facilities, and a convenience store.
- **Cost:** RV sites start at $55 per night, tent sites at $30 per night.
- **Booking Tips:** Reservations are recommended, especially during peak seasons, to ensure a spot.

4. Canyon Mesa Country Club

- **Overview:** A budget-friendly option in the Village of Oak Creek, offering condo-style accommodations perfect for families or groups.
- **Why Go:** It provides more space and amenities than a standard motel, including a fully equipped kitchen.
- **Amenities:** Outdoor pool, hot tub, tennis courts, and BBQ facilities.
- **Cost:** Rates start at $80 per night for studios, with one-bedroom condos priced around $120 per night.
- **Booking Tips:** Book early, especially for weekends, to get the best rates.

5. Oak Creek Terrace Resort

- **Overview:** An affordable and picturesque lodge along Oak Creek, offering cozy rooms and great access to outdoor activities.
- **Why Go:** It's a charming spot for those looking to experience Sedona's natural beauty at a lower cost.
- **Amenities:** Picnic areas, fishing access, and private balconies with views of the creek.
- **Cost:** Rooms start at $70 per night.
- **Booking Tips:** Request a room near the creek for a serene stay.

6. The Wildflower Inn

- **Overview:** A family-run motel located just outside Sedona, offering clean rooms at budget-friendly rates.
- **Why Go:** It's a great choice for travelers looking for a basic but comfortable place to rest after a day of exploring Sedona.
- **Amenities:** Free parking, Wi-Fi, and access to the seasonal outdoor pool.
- **Cost:** Rooms start at $60 per night.
- **Booking Tips:** Call ahead to inquire about special discounts, especially for longer stays.

These budget-friendly accommodations provide a range of options for travelers looking to enjoy Sedona without breaking the bank. Whether you prefer a hostel's social vibe, a motel's convenience, or a camping spot's closeness to nature, there's something for everyone. Book early, especially during peak seasons, to secure the best rates and accommodations.

Vacation Rentals and Unique Lodgings

Sedona offers a variety of unique lodging options perfect for travelers looking to experience a more intimate and memorable stay. Here's a list of six vacation rentals and unique lodgings, complete with details on their amenities, costs, and reasons why they might be a great fit for your Sedona adventure.

1. Sedona Treehouse

- **Overview:** A secluded treehouse perched high in the trees, offering stunning views of the red rocks and a true sense of solitude.
- **Why Go:** Ideal for couples or solo travelers seeking a romantic escape or a quiet retreat. The treehouse experience combines luxury with nature.
- **Amenities:** Private deck, hot tub, kitchenette, and a cozy living area.
- **Cost:** The treehouse rents for around $300 per night.
- **Booking Tips:** Advance booking is essential, especially for weekend stays, as this is a popular option for honeymooners.

2. Adobe Village Graham Inn

- **Overview:** A charming adobe-style bed and breakfast located near Cathedral Rock, offering an authentic Sedona experience.
- **Why Go:** It's perfect for those who enjoy the personalized touch of a B&B. The peaceful setting and proximity to hiking trails make it an excellent choice for nature lovers.
- **Amenities:** En-suite rooms with private patios, full breakfast, and a shared living area with a fireplace.
- **Cost:** Rooms start at $200 per night.
- **Booking Tips:** Book early for the best room options; the Orchid Suite, with its private entrance, is particularly popular.

3. Sky Ranch Lodge

- **Overview:** A historic lodge situated on a hilltop with sweeping views of Sedona's iconic red rocks.
- **Why Go:** It's a unique experience offering both rustic charm and modern amenities. The lodge's cabins provide a cozy, laid-back atmosphere.
- **Amenities:** Heated outdoor pool, on-site restaurant, and well-appointed rooms.
- **Cost:** Rooms range from $180 to $300 per night, depending on the cabin's proximity to the main lodge.
- **Booking Tips:** Choose a room facing west for the best sunset views.

4. The Sedona Dwellings

- **Overview:** These contemporary, eco-friendly vacation rentals are located in West Sedona. They blend seamlessly with the natural surroundings, offering peace and tranquility.
- **Why Go:** They are perfect for those wanting a more private stay with modern amenities like hot tubs and outdoor showers.
- **Amenities:** Fully equipped kitchens, private decks with outdoor seating, and lush gardens.
- **Cost:** Rentals start at $250 per night.
- **Booking Tips:** Book well in advance as they book up quickly, especially during the fall.

5. The Pink Adobe

- **Overview:** An iconic, restored 1950s cottage in the heart of Sedona's Uptown district.
- **Why Go:** This quirky little cottage offers a nostalgic charm with all the modern comforts, ideal for travelers wanting to experience Sedona's vibrant arts scene.
- **Amenities:** Full kitchen, private patio, and a cozy living room with a fireplace.
- **Cost:** Rates start at $180 per night.
- **Booking Tips:** Perfect for couples looking for a unique place to stay that's close to shops and galleries.

6. The Sedona Guest House

- **Overview:** A cozy guest house nestled in the trees, offering a serene and private environment.
- **Why Go:** This is an excellent option for travelers seeking a home-like atmosphere, ideal for families or small groups.
- **Amenities:** Three bedrooms, two baths, a full kitchen, and a spacious living area.
- **Cost:** The guest house rents for around $350 per night.
- **Booking Tips:** Ideal for those planning to stay for a week or more, as the longer you book, the better the rate.

These unique lodging options provide an exceptional and memorable experience in Sedona, allowing travelers to enjoy the area's natural beauty and cultural richness in a more private and intimate setting. Whether you prefer the charm of a historic B&B, the seclusion of a treehouse, or the comfort of a modern vacation rental, there's a perfect fit for every traveler's needs and budget.

Exploring Sedona

Chapter 7: Iconic Landmarks and Natural Wonders

Sedona is a treasure trove of natural beauty, with its red rock formations, lush canyons, and serene landscapes. Among the most iconic landmarks, Cathedral Rock stands out as a must-visit. This majestic red sandstone formation is one of the most photographed spots in Sedona, drawing visitors from around the world. Whether you're a hiker, a photographer, or simply someone looking to connect with nature, Cathedral Rock offers a breathtaking experience.

Cathedral Rock

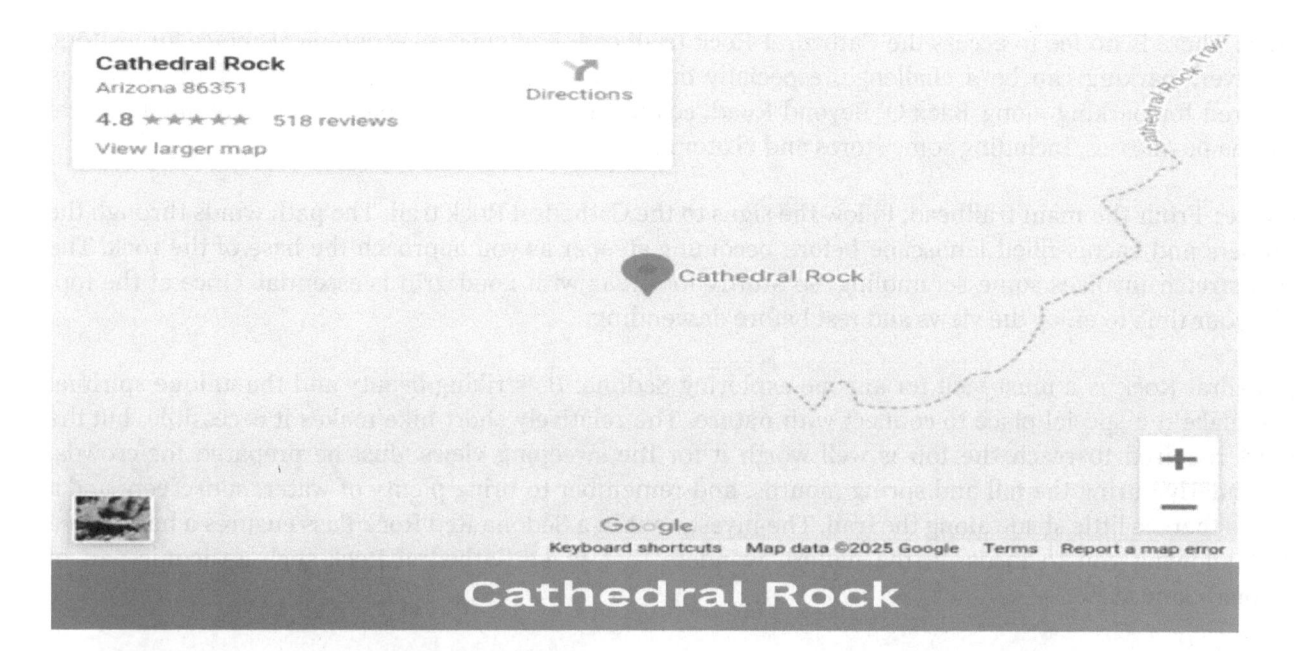

SCAN THE QR CODE

1. Open your device's camera app.
2. Point the camera at the QR code.
3. Hold steady and wait for recognition.
4. Review the displayed information.
5. Follow the prompt to access the content.

Why Go: Cathedral Rock is not just a landmark; it's an experience. The towering red spires seem to pierce the sky, making it a place of immense natural beauty and spiritual significance. The location is often considered sacred, and many people come here to meditate and connect with the earth. The sight of the sun setting over Cathedral Rock is particularly magical, with the rocks glowing a vibrant red against the darkening sky.

How to Access: The primary trailhead for Cathedral Rock is located off Back O' Beyond Road, just south of Sedona's Uptown district. The hike to the base of Cathedral Rock is relatively short but steep, making it accessible to most hikers but challenging for those not used to steep climbs. The trailhead can be crowded, especially during peak times, so arriving early in the morning is advisable to avoid the crowds.

Best Views and Photography Tips: The best views are achieved from the base of the rock formation or from the top, which requires scrambling over some rocks. The top of Cathedral Rock offers a panoramic view of Sedona's red rocks, Verde Valley, and the surrounding desert. For photographers, the best light is early morning or late afternoon when the sun casts long shadows and highlights the red rock's textures. Avoid midday, as the harsh light can wash out the colors. Use a wide-angle lens to capture the vast landscape and a tripod to stabilize your shots. The reflections on Oak Creek, which flows at the base of the rock, can add a magical element to your photos.

Cost: There is no fee to access the Cathedral Rock trailhead, making it an economical choice for visitors. However, parking can be a challenge, especially during busy periods. The Sedona Red Rock Pass is required for parking along Back O' Beyond Road, costing $5 per day. This pass can be obtained at local Sedona businesses, including some stores and visitor centers.

Route: From the main trailhead, follow the signs to the Cathedral Rock trail. The path winds through the junipers and cactus-filled landscape before becoming steeper as you approach the base of the rock. The final stretch involves some scrambling, so sturdy footwear with good grip is essential. Once at the top, take your time to enjoy the views and rest before descending.

Cathedral Rock is a must-visit for anyone exploring Sedona. Its striking beauty and the unique spiritual vibe make it a special place to connect with nature. The relatively short hike makes it accessible, but the effort required to reach the top is well worth it for the sweeping views. Just be prepared for crowds, particularly during the fall and spring months, and remember to bring plenty of water, sunscreen, and a hat, as there is little shade along the trail. The investment in a Sedona Red Rock Pass ensures a hassle-free visit, allowing you to focus on the natural wonders that make Cathedral Rock such an iconic part of Sedona's landscape.

Devil's Bridge

Why Go: Devil's Bridge is special because it provides a rare opportunity to stand on a natural rock bridge with breathtaking views of the surrounding red rocks and canyons. The bridge itself is a stunning formation, with the rock arch appearing to float in the air above the landscape. The site is a must-visit for anyone wanting to experience Sedona's dramatic scenery up close. Whether you're a hiker, photographer, or someone just looking for a memorable outdoor experience, Devil's Bridge offers something for everyone.

How to Access: The trailhead for Devil's Bridge is located off Dry Creek Road, about a 30-minute drive from Sedona's Uptown district. The trail to the bridge is moderately strenuous, about 4.2 miles round-trip, with an elevation gain of about 500 feet. The first half of the trail meanders through juniper forests, offering shade, before opening up to the red rock landscape as you approach the bridge. The trail is well-marked and easy to follow, but it can be rocky and uneven in places, so wearing sturdy hiking shoes with good ankle support is essential.

Best Views and Photography Tips: The best time to visit Devil's Bridge is early in the morning or late in the afternoon when the light is softer, and the shadows add depth to the landscape. The arch itself is the perfect focal point for photographers, with the surrounding red rocks providing a stunning backdrop. To capture the arch without too many people, arrive at the trailhead early—before 8 AM if possible. Bring a tripod for long-exposure shots and to keep your camera steady on windy days. For those willing to climb up onto the bridge, the view from the top is even more spectacular, offering sweeping vistas of the surrounding wilderness.

Cost: There is no fee to access the Devil's Bridge trailhead, which is a big plus. However, parking can be a challenge, especially during peak times. The Sedona Red Rock Pass is required for parking along Dry Creek Road, costing $5 per day. These passes can be purchased at local stores, gas stations, and visitor centers around Sedona. Arriving early in the morning will help you snag one of the limited parking spots closer to the trailhead, which is especially important in summer when the area can get very crowded.

Route: The trail begins with a gentle climb through the forest, offering occasional views of the surrounding red rock formations. After about a mile, the trail becomes steeper and rockier as you leave the shade of the forest behind. As you near the bridge, the path opens up to the dramatic red rock landscape that Sedona is famous for. The final approach involves some scrambling over rocks, but the views are worth it. Once you reach the bridge, you can either walk across it for a truly unforgettable experience or stand on the edge for some amazing photos. The return hike follows the same trail, making for a rewarding loop.

Devil's Bridge is one of Sedona's most iconic landmarks, offering both beauty and adventure. The hike to the bridge is moderate enough for most visitors but still offers a sense of accomplishment upon reaching the top. The scenery along the way is stunning, and the arch itself is a true marvel of nature. Just be prepared for crowds, especially in the spring and fall, and consider visiting on a weekday if possible. The Sedona Red Rock Pass ensures a hassle-free parking experience and allows you to focus on enjoying the natural wonders of Devil's Bridge.

Bell Rock

Why Go: Bell Rock is an iconic landmark in Sedona, easily recognizable by its bell-shaped formation jutting out from the landscape. It's a place where you can feel the ancient energy of the red rocks, making it a popular spot for both spiritual seekers and outdoor enthusiasts. The rock formation itself resembles a massive bell, standing tall amidst the surrounding red rock landscape. The area is not only beautiful but also historically significant, with ancient indigenous people having considered this spot sacred. Whether you're looking to hike, meditate, or simply enjoy the views, Bell Rock offers something for everyone.

How to Access: The trailhead for Bell Rock is located off Highway 179, about a 15-minute drive from Sedona's Uptown district. The trail to the base of Bell Rock is well-marked and easily accessible, making it a great choice for families, beginners, and anyone looking for a short hike. The trail is relatively flat for the first mile, winding through desert vegetation before it begins to ascend towards the base of the rock. The hike can be as short or as long as you want it to be, with various trails leading up different parts of Bell Rock's slopes.

Best Views and Photography Tips: The best views of Bell Rock are from the base and from the higher vantage points along the trail. For photographers, early morning or late afternoon light offers the best shots, casting long shadows and highlighting the rock's vibrant colors. To get the most out of your photos, arrive early to avoid the crowds, especially during weekends and holidays when the area can get quite busy. A wide-angle lens is ideal for capturing the expanse of the landscape, but a telephoto lens is also useful for close-ups of the rock formations and the surrounding flora. For those willing to scramble up some of the rock faces, the views from higher up on Bell Rock are even more rewarding, offering a panoramic view of the red rock country.

Cost: There is no fee to access the Bell Rock trailhead, which is a significant advantage. However, parking can be limited, especially during peak times.

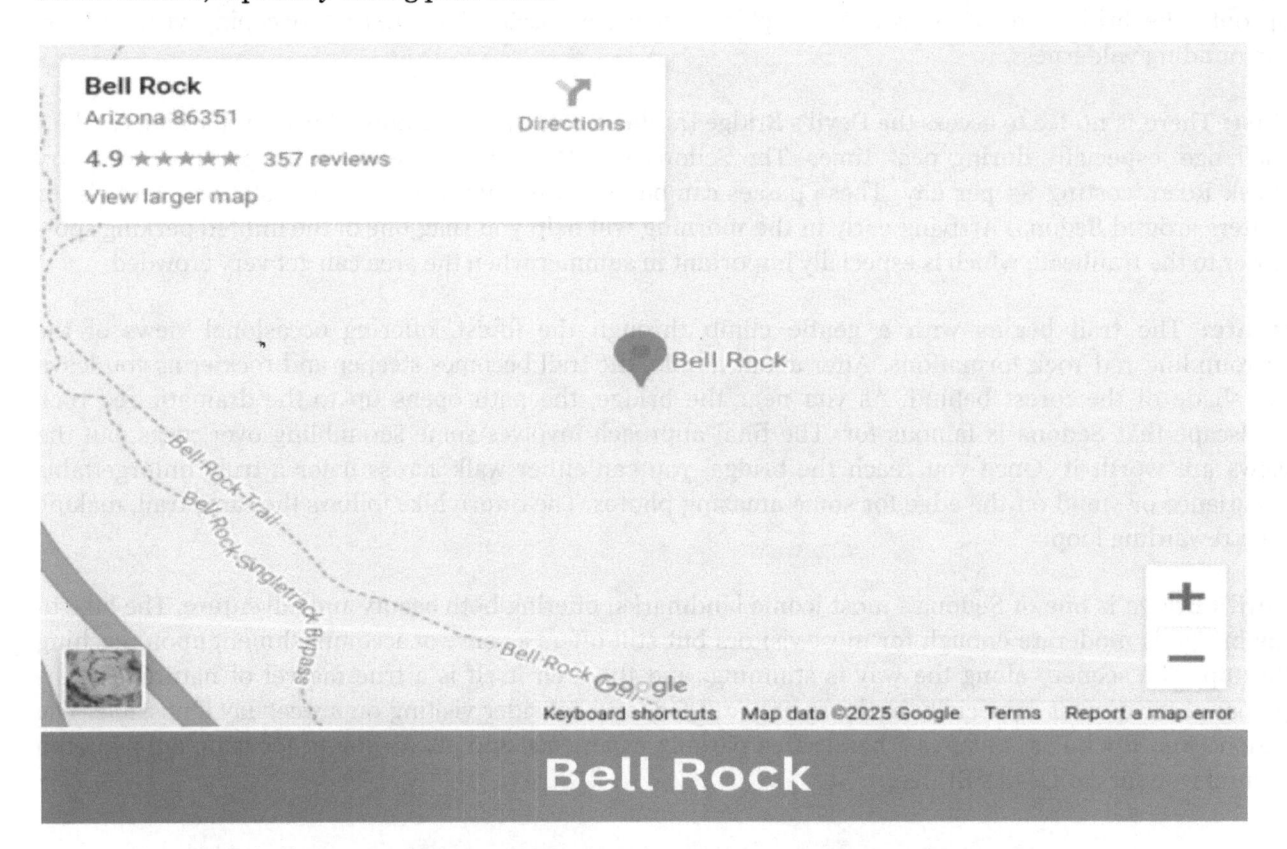

Bell Rock
Arizona 86351
4.9 ★★★★★ 357 reviews
View larger map
Directions

Bell Rock

SCAN THE QR CODE

1. Open your device's camera app.
2. Point the camera at the QR code.
3. Hold steady and wait for recognition.
4. Review the displayed information.
5. Follow the prompt to access the content.

The Sedona Red Rock Pass is required for parking along Highway 179, costing $5 per day. These passes are available at local stores, gas stations, and visitor centers in Sedona. Arriving early or later in the day increases your chances of finding a spot closer to the trailhead, which can save time and energy, particularly in the hotter months.

Route: The trail to Bell Rock begins with a flat walk through desert scrub, gradually becoming steeper as you approach the base of the rock. The first half-mile is easy and accessible, perfect for a quick jaunt. As you ascend, the terrain becomes rockier and requires some minor scrambling, which adds excitement to the hike. There are several paths that lead to the top of Bell Rock, offering different perspectives and levels of difficulty. For the most panoramic views, aim for the top, which requires a bit of climbing but is well worth the effort. The return hike follows the same route, providing a loop that's both scenic and satisfying.

Bell Rock is a quintessential Sedona experience, combining natural beauty with a sense of adventure. Its distinctive shape and serene surroundings make it a favorite among visitors. The accessibility of the trail makes it a great choice for all levels of hikers, from families to seasoned adventurers. The Sedona Red Rock Pass ensures a smooth parking experience, allowing you to focus on the natural wonders that Bell Rock offers. Whether you're there for the views, the history, or the energy of the place, Bell Rock is a must-visit in Sedona.

Oak Creek Canyon and Slide Rock State Park

Why Go: Oak Creek Canyon is a scenic canyon located along State Route 89A, about a 15-minute drive from Sedona. It's known for its lush vegetation, crystal-clear creek, and towering red rock cliffs. The area is incredibly picturesque and offers a serene escape from the hustle and bustle of Sedona. The canyon is often referred to as "America's Little Grand Canyon" due to its striking beauty and dramatic rock formations. The cool waters of Oak Creek provide a perfect retreat during the hot summer months, making it a popular destination for both swimming and hiking. Nearby Slide Rock State Park, on the other hand, offers a natural water slide, making it a fun and family-friendly spot to visit.

How to Access: Oak Creek Canyon is easily accessible from Sedona via State Route 89A, which winds through the canyon and provides breathtaking views the entire way. There are several pull-offs along the route where you can stop to take in the scenery or explore the area. One of the best ways to experience the canyon is to drive through it and stop at the viewpoints along the way. Slide Rock State Park, located at the base of Oak Creek Canyon, is accessible via the same route. The park is about a 15-minute drive from Sedona. The entrance to Slide Rock State Park is well-marked, with a small fee for parking. The park opens early in the morning and typically gets crowded by midday, so arriving early is advisable to secure a good spot.

Best Views and Photography Tips: The drive through Oak Creek Canyon offers some of the best views in Sedona. Stop at the viewpoints like Midgley Bridge for panoramic shots of the canyon and the creek below. For photographers, the early morning light is ideal for capturing the golden glow on the red rock cliffs, while late afternoon offers softer light and longer shadows that enhance the natural beauty of the area. Slide Rock State Park itself is best visited on a sunny day when the water is clear and the red rocks of the creek bed are visible. For photography, try to visit in the morning or late afternoon to avoid harsh midday light. Long exposures can be used to capture the motion of the water in the creek, creating a dreamy effect in your photos.

Cost: There is a $20 fee per vehicle to enter Slide Rock State Park, which includes access to the park's facilities and natural waterslides. This fee is collected at the entrance and is a flat rate regardless of the number of passengers in the vehicle. Parking is limited, so consider arriving early to secure a spot. For Oak Creek Canyon, there is no entrance fee for the viewpoints along State Route 89A, but parking can be tight, especially during peak times in the summer. The Sedona Red Rock Pass is required for parking at certain pull-offs and trailheads along this route, costing $5 per day. The pass is available at local stores and visitor centers in Sedona.

Route: To explore Oak Creek Canyon, simply drive along State Route 89A through the canyon. There are numerous pull-offs where you can park and explore the area on foot.

Oak Creek Canyon

SCAN THE QR CODE

1. Open your device's camera app.
2. Point the camera at the QR code.
3. Hold steady and wait for recognition.
4. Review the displayed information.
5. Follow the prompt to access the content.

The road is well-maintained and offers plenty of scenic overlooks, but it can get narrow in places, especially on weekends and during the tourist season. If you're planning on hiking in the canyon, there are several trails leading into the surrounding hills, offering varying degrees of difficulty. Slide Rock State Park is located at the base of Oak Creek Canyon and is easily accessible via the same route. The park features a natural water slide created by the smooth, red rocks of the creek bed. The area is popular for swimming and picnicking, and the natural slide is a fun activity for kids and adults alike. Be prepared for crowds, particularly during summer weekends and holidays.

Oak Creek Canyon and Slide Rock State Park are must-visit destinations in Sedona, offering a mix of stunning scenery and outdoor activities. The drive through Oak Creek Canyon alone is worth the trip, with its dramatic views and natural beauty. Slide Rock State Park provides a fun and refreshing experience, especially in the summer, making it a favorite among families. The Sedona Red Rock Pass ensures a smooth parking experience and allows you to focus on enjoying the natural wonders these areas offer. Whether you're looking for a quiet hike, a scenic drive, or a day of swimming, both Oak Creek Canyon and Slide Rock State Park have something for everyone.

Red Rock Crossing and Crescent Moon Picnic Site

Red Rock Crossing

Sedona is renowned for its stunning natural beauty, and Red Rock Crossing, combined with the nearby Crescent Moon Picnic Site, is one of its most beloved spots. Having visited these areas multiple times, I can vouch for their unique charm and breathtaking views. Whether you're seeking peace and quiet, an opportunity to capture memorable photographs, or simply a place to relax, these spots have it all.

Why Go: Red Rock Crossing, located along Oak Creek, is one of the most photographed areas in Sedona, especially due to its iconic view of Cathedral Rock. This site is famous for its tranquil waters, framed by towering red rock cliffs. It's a place where you can feel deeply connected to nature, surrounded by the beauty of Sedona's iconic red rocks. Crescent Moon Picnic Site, situated a bit further up from Red Rock Crossing, is an equally delightful spot offering picnic areas, easy trails, and access to the serene waters of Oak Creek. Both sites are perfect for those seeking a peaceful retreat away from the more crowded trails in Sedona.

How to Access: To reach Red Rock Crossing, follow State Route 179 south from Sedona until you reach the junction with Red Rock Loop Road. Turn left onto Red Rock Loop Road, and follow the signs to the parking area for Red Rock Crossing. The parking area is free, but it fills up quickly, especially on weekends and holidays, so arriving early is advised. The path to the water is relatively flat and easily accessible, making it suitable for families with children and elderly visitors. The area can get crowded during the day, especially at sunrise and sunset, which are the best times for photography.

Crescent Moon Picnic Site is accessible via the same Red Rock Loop Road. It's only a short distance further from Red Rock Crossing, making it a convenient addition to your itinerary. The site includes a picnic area, restrooms, and easy trails along Oak Creek. The entry fee to Crescent Moon Picnic Site is $10 per vehicle. The site opens early and closes in the early evening, offering plenty of daylight hours to enjoy a picnic, swim, or relax by the creek. The parking area here is also limited, but it's typically less crowded than Red Rock Crossing, providing a more tranquil experience.

Best Views and Photography Tips: Red Rock Crossing is best visited during the early morning or late afternoon when the light is softer and the reflection on Oak Creek is at its most stunning. The view of Cathedral Rock from here is simply iconic; it's often depicted in Sedona postcards and travel brochures. For photographers, this spot offers numerous angles to capture the rock formation's reflection in the water. A long exposure can be used to smooth out the movement of the creek, creating a beautiful, dream-like effect.

Crescent Moon Picnic Site

Crescent Moon Picnic Site is ideal for those wanting to capture both the red rocks and the reflections on the creek. The best photography opportunities come early in the morning or late afternoon when the sunlight filters through the trees and illuminates the rocks and water. The picnic site also provides a more relaxed setting, with opportunities for family photos and landscapes that include both the natural surroundings and the picnic tables as foreground elements.

Cost: There is a $10 fee per vehicle to enter Crescent Moon Picnic Site, which is collected at the entrance. This fee includes access to the picnic area and the trails along Oak Creek. The cost is well worth it, given the serene atmosphere and beautiful setting. Red Rock Crossing is free to enter, but you'll need to pay for parking if you're staying in the lot for an extended period. There is a $5 Sedona Red Rock Pass required for parking in the designated areas along Red Rock Loop Road, which is necessary to avoid any parking violations. This pass can be purchased at local stores or visitor centers in Sedona.

Route: To explore these areas, take the Red Rock Loop Road from Sedona and follow the signs. Both Red Rock Crossing and Crescent Moon Picnic Site are accessible via this route, making them easy to incorporate into a single day's visit. The drive through Red Rock Loop Road is beautiful and provides several other hiking opportunities, so it's worth exploring further if time allows. Be aware that the road can get busy, especially during peak seasons, so plan accordingly. If you arrive early in the morning, you'll likely have the place to yourself, or at least not be surrounded by crowds. Both locations are accessible by car, with parking close to the trailheads, making them suitable for visitors of all ages and abilities.

Red Rock Crossing and Crescent Moon Picnic Site are must-visit spots in Sedona, offering some of the best views and most tranquil settings in the area. Whether you're visiting for photography, a quiet picnic, or a leisurely day by the water, these locations provide an authentic taste of Sedona's natural beauty. Arriving early to beat the crowds is key to fully enjoying these spots, especially if you're hoping to capture the perfect shot of Cathedral Rock. The Sedona Red Rock Pass is a small investment that allows you to fully enjoy these scenic areas without worrying about parking limitations.

Chapter 8: Sedona's Vortex Sites

What Are Vortexes?

Sedona is renowned not just for its stunning red rock formations and natural beauty but also for its spiritual energy and mysterious vortex sites. These vortexes have drawn spiritual seekers, healers, and energy workers from around the world, all drawn to the idea that Sedona's unique geology enhances spiritual experiences. As someone who has visited Sedona numerous times, I've come to appreciate the profound and sometimes intangible energy these vortex sites offer.

What Are Vortexes? Vortexes are believed to be swirling centers of energy located in specific areas within Sedona. The concept of a vortex is rooted in New Age spirituality, with the idea that these sites can amplify personal energy, enhance healing, and foster a deeper connection to the natural world. The name "vortex" refers to the swirling energy patterns that are said to exist in the earth at these locations. These energy centers are thought to be caused by the unique geological composition of Sedona's rocks, which includes quartz and other minerals known for their electromagnetic properties.

Sedona's vortex sites are considered sacred by many Indigenous tribes of the region. These locations are associated with spiritual and healing energies, and they are believed to help align the body's energy centers (chakras) when one meditates or simply sits quietly at these sites. Each vortex is associated with a specific type of energy — masculine or feminine — and is believed to have different properties and effects on the human spirit.

Types of Vortexes:

1. **Feminine Vortexes**: These are sites associated with nurturing, healing, and spiritual renewal. They are typically found in places that are lush, green, and have a softer, more feminine energy. For instance, Boynton Canyon is considered one of the primary feminine vortex sites in Sedona. It is surrounded by towering cliffs and features the Seven Sacred Pools, which offer a serene and peaceful energy perfect for meditation and reflection.

2. **Masculine Vortexes**: These are sites that are more active and energizing, often associated with transformation and strength. Cathedral Rock is one of the most famous masculine vortex sites. It's a place where the energy feels powerful and transformative, often described as a place for personal empowerment and spiritual growth. The rugged, steep terrain and panoramic views enhance the site's dynamic energy, making it ideal for introspection and meditation.

A Guide to Spiritual and Energetic Experiences

Experiencing Vortex Energy: Experiencing a vortex is a deeply personal journey. For some, it's an almost tangible experience, feeling a sudden rush of energy, or a sensation of being surrounded by a gentle, vibrating current. For others, the experience is more subtle, feeling a quiet sense of peace or clarity. There's no right or wrong way to connect with these energies; it's all about being open to the experience. Here's how to engage with Sedona's vortex sites:

1. **Visit with an Open Mind**: To fully experience a vortex, it's important to visit with an open heart and mind. Let go of preconceived notions and be receptive to the energies around you. Trust your instincts and allow yourself to be present in the moment.

2. **Sit or Stand Quietly**: Find a spot at the site that feels comfortable to you. Sit or stand quietly, focusing on your breath. Allow yourself to absorb the natural surroundings and feel the subtle energies around you. Some people find it helpful to close their eyes and meditate, while others prefer simply sitting in silence.

3. **Walk the Land**: Walking the land around a vortex can be a transformative experience. The energies can be felt more intensely when you move through the area, engaging with the environment. The act of walking allows the energy to flow through your body more readily, promoting relaxation and inner peace.

4. **Use Crystals**: Crystals, such as quartz, are often used at vortex sites. Many believe that placing crystals on the ground or holding them in your hand can enhance the energy exchange between yourself and the land. Choose a crystal that resonates with you and feel its energy combine with the vortex's energy.

Best Vortex Sites to Visit:

1. **Boynton Canyon**: As mentioned earlier, this site is a primary feminine vortex, surrounded by lush green vegetation and the Seven Sacred Pools. It's a perfect place for meditation and healing.

2. **Cathedral Rock**: One of the most famous masculine vortex sites, known for its powerful energy. The hike to the top is strenuous but offers incredible views and a deeply transformative experience.

3. **Airport Mesa**: Another well-known vortex site, accessible with a short hike. The views from the mesa are stunning, and the energy here is uplifting and positive, making it a great place for clearing and renewal.

4. **Red Rock Crossing**: This site offers a softer, feminine energy, making it ideal for those seeking peace and relaxation. The view of Cathedral Rock from here is particularly iconic and soothing.

Cost and Access: Vortex sites in Sedona are free to visit, though there are associated fees for parking at some locations. For instance, Airport Mesa and Cathedral Rock have designated parking areas that require the Sedona Red Rock Pass, which costs $5 per day. Boynton Canyon requires a pass for parking as well, and the cost is $5. This pass can be purchased at various locations around Sedona, such as the visitor centers or local stores.

Whether you are a seasoned energy worker or just curious about the spiritual energy Sedona has to offer, experiencing a vortex can be a profound and memorable part of your journey. The spiritual energy at these sites is palpable and offers a unique way to connect with nature and oneself. Be prepared to let go, be open to receiving, and trust the process. Each vortex has its own unique energy, so don't rush your visit; take your time to fully immerse yourself in the experience.

Chapter 9: Best Hiking Trails in Sedona

A Guide to Spiritual and Energetic Experiences

Sedona is a hiker's paradise with its stunning red rock formations, expansive desert landscapes, and a variety of trails that cater to all levels of hikers. From easy nature walks to challenging advanced hikes, Sedona offers something for everyone. Having hiked these trails multiple times, I can confidently say that each trail offers a unique experience and breathtaking views. Here's a guide to some of the best hiking trails in Sedona, with details on difficulty levels, trail lengths, and safety tips.

1. Cathedral Rock Trail (Moderate)

Trail Description: Cathedral Rock is one of the most iconic and photographed landmarks in Sedona. The trailhead begins at a small parking area just off Back O' Beyond Road. The hike to the top is challenging but manageable with frequent stops to catch your breath. The trail consists of a series of steep switchbacks that lead to the saddle between the two spires of Cathedral Rock.

Distance: The total distance from the trailhead to the saddle and back is about 1.5 miles. However, if you choose to scramble up to the summit, it adds another 0.5 miles to the hike.

Difficulty: Moderate. The trail is steep and rocky, requiring some scrambling, especially near the summit. This trail is not recommended for young children or those with a fear of heights due to the exposure.

Why Go: The payoff for completing this hike is unparalleled. At the top, you're rewarded with sweeping views of Sedona, making it one of the best spots for sunset views. The energy at the top is palpable, making it a spiritually rewarding experience.

Cost: There is a fee for parking at the Cathedral Rock trailhead, which costs $5 per day and can be paid via the Sedona Red Rock Pass. This pass can be purchased at various locations around Sedona, including visitor centers and convenience stores.

Safety Tips: Wear sturdy hiking shoes with good grip, as the trail can be slippery when wet. Carry plenty of water and snacks. It's advisable to start the hike early in the day to avoid the intense afternoon heat, especially in summer. Don't attempt the scramble to the summit in wet or rainy conditions, as the rocks can become dangerously slippery.

2. Birthing Cave Trail (Easy-Moderate)

Trail Description: The Birthing Cave Trail is a short, easy hike that leads to a small cave hidden among the rocks. The trailhead is located off Boynton Pass Road, and the hike is suitable for families and casual hikers.

Distance: About 0.6 miles round trip, making it an ideal option for those looking for a quick, scenic hike.

Difficulty: Easy to moderate. The trail is fairly flat with a gentle incline leading to the cave. There's some scrambling required at the end to reach the cave, which gives it a moderate feel.

Why Go: The trail offers incredible views of the surrounding red rock formations and a sense of tranquility in the quiet of the cave. The cave itself is a unique geological feature and offers a cool retreat on a hot day.

Cost: No fee for parking. It's accessible for all, making it a great option for families or those looking to introduce young kids to hiking.

Safety Tips: Wear appropriate footwear with good tread, as the trail can be rocky. Bring water, especially during the summer months, as it's easy to become dehydrated. Keep an eye on kids near the cave, as the entrance can be a bit tricky to navigate.

3. Devil's Bridge (Moderate-Advanced)

Trail Description: Devil's Bridge is one of the most popular hikes in Sedona. It's named after the natural sandstone arch that you can walk across. The trailhead is off Dry Creek Road and involves a strenuous ascent over loose, rocky terrain.

Distance: The round trip is about 4.2 miles, but the last 0.5 miles involves steep climbing and a scramble over slickrock to reach the bridge itself.

Difficulty: Moderate to advanced. The trail is steep and the scramble to the bridge requires a good level of physical fitness and comfort with heights.

Why Go: Devil's Bridge offers some of the most spectacular views of Sedona's red rock landscape. Walking across the bridge feels like stepping into another world, with incredible panoramas that stretch for miles. The site is particularly popular for sunset photography.

Cost: There is a $5 parking fee for the Devil's Bridge trailhead. Like other popular trailheads, this requires a Sedona Red Rock Pass.

Safety Tips: Wear sturdy hiking boots with good ankle support and tread. Carry at least a liter of water per person, as the hike is strenuous. Start early to avoid the heat and crowds, especially during peak tourist seasons. The final stretch up to the bridge involves a scramble on steep rock with minimal guardrails, so take your time and watch your footing.

4. **West Fork Oak Creek Trail (Moderate-Advanced)**

Trail Description: This trail is a Sedona favorite, offering a cool and shaded hike along Oak Creek. The trailhead is located near the Red Rock Ranger Station on Oak Creek Canyon's east side.

Distance: The full trail is about 6 miles out and back, but it can be shortened depending on where you park and turn around.

Difficulty: Moderate. The trail is relatively flat and follows the creek most of the way, but there are some rocky sections and stream crossings that can be challenging after rain.

Why Go: The West Fork Trail is ideal for those who want to escape the summer heat and enjoy a cooler, more shaded hike. The trail offers beautiful red rock scenery, lush greenery, and multiple stream crossings, making it perfect for those who enjoy a bit of adventure in their hikes.

Cost: There is a fee for parking, with costs starting at $10 for a full day. The pass can be purchased at the trailhead or online in advance.

Safety Tips: Wear waterproof shoes if hiking after rain, as the trail can become muddy. Bring hiking poles to help with the crossings and to manage the occasional rocky sections. Check the weather forecast before setting out, as the creek can swell unexpectedly during heavy rain.

5. **Soldier Pass Trail (Moderate-Advanced)**

Trail Description: The Soldier Pass Trail is a great hike that offers a mix of scenery — including arches, caves, and even ancient ruins. The trailhead is located off Soldier Pass Road.

Distance: About 4.2 miles round trip. The trail includes some steep sections and requires scrambling over rocks.

Difficulty: Moderate to advanced. The initial part of the trail is relatively easy but becomes more challenging as you approach the Arches and Devil's Kitchen sinkhole.

Why Go: This trail offers some of the best scenic diversity in Sedona. The arches and the Devil's Kitchen rock formations are unique highlights. The energy of the place is palpable, especially near the arch where many stop for meditation.

Cost: No fee for parking. This trail is accessible to the public without the need for a Red Rock Pass.

Safety Tips: Wear sturdy hiking boots to navigate the rocky sections and scrambles. Bring plenty of water and snacks, as the hike can be strenuous. The hike is best done early in the day to avoid the heat and the crowds, especially during weekends.

6. Seven Sacred Pools Trail (Easy-Moderate)

Trail Description: This is a short, scenic hike located off Boynton Canyon Road, leading to a series of small, natural pools surrounded by red rock formations.

Distance: About 1.5 miles round trip.

Difficulty: Easy to moderate. The trail is relatively flat with a few mild ups and downs but is accessible for most hikers.

Why Go: The pools are a hidden gem, offering a serene spot for relaxation and swimming, especially in the summer. The energy here is calming, making it a favorite for picnicking and meditation.

Cost: A $5 fee for parking is required. This can be paid via the Sedona Red Rock Pass at the trailhead.

Safety Tips: Wear sturdy footwear for the rocky terrain. Bring water and a hat to protect from the sun. The pools can be slippery, especially after rain, so take care around them. It's advisable to go early in the day or later in the afternoon to avoid crowds.

Sedona's hiking trails offer a diverse range of experiences, from challenging climbs to gentle strolls along scenic creeks. Each trail has its unique charm and rewards, making Sedona a top destination for hikers of all levels. Whether you're looking for panoramic views, ancient ruins, or peaceful swimming holes, there's a trail in Sedona waiting to be explored. Always be prepared for changing conditions, carry the essentials, and respect the natural environment to ensure a safe and enjoyable hike.

Chapter 10: Outdoor Adventures in Sedona

Jeep Tours, Hot Air Balloon Rides, and Mountain Biking

Sedona is not just a place to admire from a distance—it's a playground for outdoor enthusiasts. From thrilling Jeep tours that navigate the rugged red rock terrain to serene hot air balloon rides that offer unparalleled views, and exhilarating mountain biking trails, Sedona has something for everyone. With my many visits and countless adventures here, I can confidently guide you through some of the best outdoor activities, sharing tips on booking, what to expect, and how to make the most of your time.

1. Jeep Tours: Rugged Exploration of Sedona's Backcountry

Sedona's red rock landscape begs to be explored, and Jeep tours are one of the best ways to dive deep into the rugged beauty of the area. Local companies like **Pink Jeep Tours**, **Red Rock Jeep Tours**, and **Safari Jeep Tours** offer expertly guided excursions.

- **Why Go**: Jeep tours allow you to access remote areas that would be impossible to reach on foot, such as Schnebly Hill Road, Broken Arrow Trail, and Diamondback Gulch. These tours are packed with adventure and often include fascinating historical and geological commentary from knowledgeable guides.
- **Cost**: Prices range from $95 to $150 per person, depending on the tour's length and destination. Private tours can be arranged for a more exclusive experience, usually starting at $400.
- **What to Expect**: The rides can be bumpy and exhilarating, especially on trails like Broken Arrow. You'll stop at scenic viewpoints for photos, and many tours offer detailed explanations of Sedona's vortex energy sites. Tours typically last 1.5 to 3 hours.

Tips:

- Book your tour in advance, especially during peak seasons (spring and fall).
- Wear comfortable clothing and sturdy shoes, as some tours may include short walks.
- Bring water, sunscreen, and a camera to capture the stunning landscapes.

2. Hot Air Balloon Rides: Sunrise Serenity Over Sedona

Few experiences in Sedona compare to the serenity and awe of a hot air balloon ride. Companies like **Red Rock Balloons** and **Northern Light Balloon Expeditions** offer sunrise flights that provide panoramic views of the iconic red rock formations and Verde Valley.

- **Why Go**: A hot air balloon ride offers a peaceful yet thrilling perspective of Sedona. The early morning light enhances the vibrant reds and oranges of the rocks, creating a magical experience. It's also an opportunity to see wildlife such as deer or coyotes from above.
- **Cost**: The cost typically ranges from $250 to $300 per person. Most packages include a post-flight champagne toast and light breakfast.
- **What to Expect**: Flights begin at sunrise, requiring an early start—pickups often occur between 4:30 and 5:30 a.m. The ride itself lasts about 1 to 1.5 hours. The gentle ascent and descent make this an activity suitable for most, even those with a slight fear of heights.

Tips:

- Dress in layers, as mornings can be chilly, but temperatures warm quickly once the sun rises.

- Wear sturdy, closed-toe shoes, as you'll need to navigate uneven ground during the launch and landing.
- Check cancellation policies, as flights are weather-dependent and can be rescheduled.

3. Mountain Biking: Thrills on Two Wheels

Sedona is a world-class mountain biking destination, offering trails for every skill level. Whether you're a beginner looking for scenic routes or an experienced rider seeking adrenaline-pumping challenges, Sedona delivers. Popular trailheads include **Bell Rock Pathway**, **Chuckwagon Trail**, and **Hiline Trail**.

- **Why Go**: Sedona's trails wind through breathtaking landscapes, from smooth single-track paths to technical descents. The dramatic red rock formations provide a stunning backdrop, and the well-maintained trails are designed to suit riders of all abilities.
- **Cost**: Renting a mountain bike costs around $50 to $100 per day, depending on the type of bike. Guided tours range from $100 to $200 per person. Rentals and tours are available from local shops like **Sedona Bike & Bean** and **Over the Edge Sedona**.
- **What to Expect**: Beginners can enjoy easier trails like Bell Rock Pathway, a 3.5-mile round-trip route with gentle inclines and sweeping views. Intermediate and advanced riders will love trails like Mescal and Hiline, which offer technical challenges and heart-stopping descents. Many trails have features like slickrock sections, narrow ledges, and rock gardens.

Tips:

- Always wear a helmet and consider additional protective gear, especially for advanced trails.
- Carry plenty of water and snacks, as hydration is crucial in Sedona's dry climate.
- Study trail maps before heading out and consider downloading the Trailforks app for real-time navigation.

Practical Advice for Booking and Safety

Booking Tips:

- Book Jeep tours and hot air balloon rides at least two weeks in advance during peak seasons. For mountain biking, reserve high-quality rental bikes ahead of time, especially if you have specific preferences.
- Look for packages that combine activities if you're planning multiple adventures, as this can save money.

General Safety Tips:

- Be aware of the weather, as sudden storms can occur, particularly during monsoon season (July–September).
- Always carry plenty of water, sunscreen, and a hat, no matter the activity.
- Let someone know your plans, especially for mountain biking on remote trails.

Sedona's outdoor adventures provide a perfect balance of adrenaline, serenity, and connection to nature. With proper planning and the right mindset, you'll create memories that last a lifetime while exploring this incredible landscape. Whether you're scaling rugged terrain, floating peacefully above the desert, or navigating thrilling bike trails, Sedona promises an unforgettable adventure.

Chapter 11: Sedona's Art Scene

Must-Visit Galleries and Studios

Sedona's rich artistic legacy stems from its unparalleled natural beauty, which has inspired countless artists, sculptors, and creators over the years. With its vibrant art galleries and studios, Sedona offers visitors an opportunity to experience the convergence of natural wonder and human creativity. Having explored Sedona's art scene extensively, I can vouch for the transformative experience of immersing yourself in its artistic offerings. Below are six must-visit galleries and studios that encapsulate Sedona's role in the art world.

1. Tlaquepaque Arts and Shopping Village
Location: 336 AZ-179, Sedona, AZ 86336
Why Go: Tlaquepaque, modeled after a traditional Mexican village, is the heart of Sedona's art scene. Its cobblestone paths and vine-covered courtyards create a tranquil setting for over 50 specialty shops, galleries, and working studios. The galleries showcase diverse works, from contemporary paintings to Navajo weavings and hand-blown glass.
Must-See: Rowe Fine Art Gallery and Kuivato Glass Art Gallery.
Cost: Free to enter, but artwork ranges from $50 for prints to $10,000+ for original pieces.
Tips: Plan your visit during the weekday mornings to avoid crowds and meet artists working in their studios.

2. Sedona Arts Center
Location: 15 Art Barn Rd, Sedona, AZ 86336
Why Go: Founded in 1958, the Sedona Arts Center is a cornerstone of the town's cultural heritage. It houses a rotating gallery featuring works from local and regional artists and offers workshops and classes for all skill levels.
Must-See: The Fine Art Gallery showcases paintings, sculptures, ceramics, and jewelry, many inspired by Sedona's landscapes.
Cost: Free entry; workshops start at $50 for beginner classes.
Tips: Check their calendar for live demonstrations and artist talks. If you're a collector, this is a great place to find unique, locally made pieces.

3. Exposures International Gallery of Fine Art
Location: 561 AZ-179, Sedona, AZ 86336
Why Go: Known as one of the largest fine art galleries in the Southwest, Exposures International is a feast for the senses. Spanning 20,000 square feet, the gallery features everything from intricate bronze sculptures to bold abstract paintings.
Must-See: The outdoor sculpture garden and contemporary glass art displays.
Cost: Free to visit; art pieces range from $1,000 to $50,000.
Tips: Even if you're not purchasing, the gallery's stunning layout and curated collection make it worth a visit.

4. Goldenstein Gallery
Location: 150 AZ-179, Sedona, AZ 86336
Why Go: Voted Sedona's Best Gallery for over a decade, Goldenstein Gallery is renowned for its diverse collection and emphasis on showcasing emerging talent. Its displays rotate frequently, ensuring there's always something new to discover.
Must-See: The gallery's "Art in the Landscape" installations, where sculptures are placed outdoors to

blend with Sedona's red rock surroundings.

Cost: Free entry; artworks are priced between $500 and $25,000.

Tips: Visit during one of their monthly artist receptions to meet creators and gain deeper insights into their works.

5. Renee Taylor Gallery

Location: 336 AZ-179, Sedona, AZ 86336

Why Go: Specializing in modern and contemporary art, Renee Taylor Gallery is perfect for those with a taste for sleek, minimalist designs. The gallery's focus on fine jewelry, kinetic wind sculptures, and innovative home décor makes it stand out.

Must-See: Kinetic sculptures by artist Lyman Whitaker, which are mesmerizing when viewed against Sedona's natural backdrop.

Cost: Free to browse; prices range from $200 for smaller sculptures to $20,000+ for large installations.

Tips: Take your time exploring the outdoor displays, especially on windy days when the sculptures are in motion.

6. Gallery of Modern Masters

Location: 671 AZ-179, Sedona, AZ 86336

Why Go: This gallery specializes in contemporary fine art and glasswork. The vibrant collection includes everything from fused glass creations to surrealist paintings, appealing to modern art enthusiasts.

Must-See: Stunning glass sculptures and mixed media pieces that catch and play with Sedona's natural light.

Cost: Free entry; art prices range from $100 for prints to $15,000 for original works.

Tips: The staff is incredibly knowledgeable and can provide detailed insights into the techniques and stories behind the pieces.

Sedona's art scene is more than just a collection of galleries—it's a testament to the town's ability to inspire and nurture creativity. With its stunning landscapes and vibrant energy, Sedona has long attracted artists seeking to capture its essence in their work. Visiting these galleries not only supports local artists but also provides a deeper connection to Sedona's unique spirit. Whether you're an avid collector, a casual browser, or someone seeking inspiration, Sedona's art scene offers a rich and rewarding experience.

Chapter 12: Historical and Cultural Landmarks

Chapel of the Holy Cross, Palatki Heritage Site, and More

Sedona is not just a haven for outdoor enthusiasts; it's also rich in history and culture, offering landmarks that connect visitors to its spiritual, artistic, and ancient roots. As someone who has explored these sites multiple times, I can assure you they provide a fascinating window into Sedona's multifaceted identity.

1. Chapel of the Holy Cross
Location: 780 Chapel Rd, Sedona, AZ 86336
Why Go: Perched dramatically against Sedona's red rock cliffs, the Chapel of the Holy Cross is a marvel of modern architecture and a spiritual haven. Designed in the 1950s by Marguerite Brunswig Staude, the chapel blends seamlessly into the natural landscape, offering breathtaking views and a sense of serenity. Inside, the minimalist design directs your focus to the massive floor-to-ceiling windows overlooking Sedona's iconic rock formations, including Bell Rock and Cathedral Rock.
How to Access: The chapel is located just off Highway 179, and parking is free. There is a short but steep paved walkway leading to the chapel, so comfortable footwear is recommended.
Cost: Entry is free, but donations are appreciated.
Tips for Visitors: Visit early in the morning or late afternoon to avoid crowds and to see the red rocks bathed in soft, golden light—ideal for photography.

2. Palatki Heritage Site
Location: 10290 N Forest Rd 795, Sedona, AZ 86336
Why Go: The Palatki Heritage Site is a fascinating archaeological treasure, showcasing ancient cliff dwellings and rock art left by the Sinagua people over 800 years ago. This site offers a glimpse into the lives of Sedona's earliest inhabitants and their connection to the land. Guided tours by knowledgeable rangers provide in-depth insights into the history and significance of the site.
How to Access: From Sedona, take Highway 89A to Forest Road 525. The last stretch is a dirt road but accessible by most vehicles. Reservations are required and can be made through the Red Rock Ranger District.
Cost: $10 per vehicle or free with an America the Beautiful Pass.
Tips for Visitors: Bring water and wear sturdy shoes, as the trail to the ruins is uneven. Midday visits offer the best lighting for photographing the ancient petroglyphs.

3. Sedona Heritage Museum
Location: 735 Jordan Rd, Sedona, AZ 86336
Why Go: Located in Jordan Historical Park, the Sedona Heritage Museum chronicles the town's early days as a pioneer settlement. Exhibits focus on the history of farming, ranching, and filmmaking in the area, with fascinating artifacts and personal stories from Sedona's earliest residents. The museum also hosts seasonal events, including the annual Apple Festival.
How to Access: The museum is easily accessible from downtown Sedona, with ample parking available.
Cost: Admission is $7 for adults, $3 for children ages 6–12, and free for children under 6.
Tips for Visitors: Plan your visit during one of their living history demonstrations to see blacksmithing and other pioneer-era crafts in action.

4. Amitabha Stupa and Peace Park
Location: 2650 Pueblo Dr, Sedona, AZ 86336
Why Go: A tranquil site for reflection and meditation, the Amitabha Stupa is a spiritual landmark nestled among Sedona's red rocks. This 36-foot-tall Buddhist structure is surrounded by peaceful trails

and prayer flags, offering a serene retreat for those seeking spiritual renewal. It's an ideal spot to take a break from Sedona's bustling tourist areas.

How to Access: The site is a short drive from Highway 89A and features a free parking lot. The stupa is accessible via a short, uphill dirt path.

Cost: Free, though donations are encouraged to support the upkeep of the park.

Tips for Visitors: Visit during sunrise or sunset for a truly magical experience. Silence is requested on-site to maintain the tranquil atmosphere.

5. V-Bar-V Heritage Site

Location: 6750 AZ-179, Rimrock, AZ 86335 (approximately 20 minutes south of Sedona)

Why Go: Home to one of the best-preserved and largest collections of petroglyphs in Arizona, the V-Bar-V Heritage Site showcases more than 1,000 ancient symbols carved into sandstone by the Sinagua people. These petroglyphs are thought to represent a solar calendar, adding to the site's archaeological intrigue.

How to Access: Located just off Highway 179, the site is accessible via a flat half-mile trail from the parking lot.

Cost: $5 per vehicle or free with an America the Beautiful Pass.

Tips for Visitors: Arrive early to join a ranger-led tour and gain detailed insights into the petroglyphs' significance.

6. Honanki Heritage Site

Location: 1156 Loy Butte Rd, Sedona, AZ 86336

Why Go: Another incredible archaeological site, Honanki offers well-preserved cliff dwellings and pictographs from the Sinagua people. This site is less crowded than Palatki, making it a more intimate experience for history buffs.

How to Access: Located off Forest Road 525, the dirt road leading to Honanki requires a high-clearance vehicle. Guided tours are available through Pink Jeep Tours.

Cost: $10 per vehicle or free with an America the Beautiful Pass.

Tips for Visitors: Combine your visit with Palatki for a full day of exploring Sedona's ancient history.

Sedona's historical and cultural landmarks offer a captivating journey through time, from ancient civilizations to modern spirituality. Whether you're marveling at ancient petroglyphs, finding peace at a Buddhist stupa, or exploring Sedona's pioneering past, these sites provide a deeper appreciation of the region's rich heritage.

Historical Significance and Visitor Information

Sedona is a region steeped in historical and cultural significance, where ancient civilizations, pioneering settlers, and modern spiritual seekers have all left their mark. From the intricate cliff dwellings of the Sinagua people to the architectural masterpiece of the Chapel of the Holy Cross, each site tells a unique story of the land and its people. Here's an in-depth guide to the historical significance of Sedona's iconic landmarks and practical visitor information to ensure a fulfilling trip.

Chapel of the Holy Cross

Historical Significance: Completed in 1956, the Chapel of the Holy Cross stands as a testament to spiritual devotion and architectural ingenuity. Commissioned by local artist Marguerite Brunswig Staude, who was inspired by the Empire State Building, the chapel symbolizes harmony between human creativity and nature. Its location amidst the towering red rocks highlights Sedona's reputation as a spiritual hub.

Visitor Information:

- **Location**: 780 Chapel Rd, Sedona, AZ 86336
- **Cost**: Free entry; donations are welcomed.
- **Hours**: Open daily from 9 a.m. to 5 p.m.
- **Tips**: Visit early in the morning for fewer crowds and golden hour photography. Parking is limited, so plan accordingly.

Palatki Heritage Site

Historical Significance: The Palatki Heritage Site is a UNESCO-recognized location showcasing ancient cliff dwellings and rock art created by the Sinagua people, who thrived in the area between 1150 and 1350 CE. The petroglyphs and pictographs provide invaluable insights into their culture, spiritual beliefs, and daily life.

Visitor Information:

- **Location**: 10290 N Forest Rd 795, Sedona, AZ 86336
- **Cost**: $10 per vehicle; free with an America the Beautiful Pass.
- **Hours**: Open daily from 9:30 a.m. to 3 p.m.; reservations required for tours.
- **Tips**: Bring water, wear sturdy shoes, and consider visiting during cooler months to fully enjoy the trails and guided tours.

Sedona Heritage Museum

Historical Significance: Housed in a former pioneer family's homestead, the Sedona Heritage Museum offers a glimpse into Sedona's transition from a ranching and farming community to a renowned tourist destination. Exhibits include artifacts from Sedona's early settlers, details on its role in Hollywood filmmaking, and accounts of Native American history.

Visitor Information:

- **Location**: 735 Jordan Rd, Sedona, AZ 86336
- **Cost**: $7 for adults, $3 for children ages 6–12, free for children under 6.
- **Hours**: Open daily from 11 a.m. to 3 p.m.
- **Tips**: Allocate at least an hour to explore the exhibits. Combine your visit with a walk through the scenic Jordan Historical Park.

Amitabha Stupa and Peace Park

Historical Significance: Built in 2004, the Amitabha Stupa is a sacred Buddhist structure designed to promote healing, harmony, and spiritual enlightenment. Named after Buddha Amitabha, it draws spiritual seekers from around the world and serves as a focal point for meditation and prayer.

Visitor Information:

- **Location**: 2650 Pueblo Dr, Sedona, AZ 86336
- **Cost**: Free, though donations are appreciated.
- **Hours**: Open daily from dawn to dusk.
- **Tips**: Wear comfortable shoes for the dirt trails and bring a journal for reflection. Visit at sunrise or sunset for a more serene experience.

V-Bar-V Heritage Site

Historical Significance: The V-Bar-V Heritage Site features one of the largest and best-preserved collections of petroglyphs in Arizona. Created by the Sinagua people, these ancient carvings depict celestial patterns and may have served as an agricultural calendar.

Visitor Information:

- **Location**: 6750 AZ-179, Rimrock, AZ 86335
- **Cost**: $5 per vehicle; free with an America the Beautiful Pass.
- **Hours**: Open Thursday through Sunday from 9:30 a.m. to 3 p.m.
- **Tips**: Arrive early to join a ranger-led tour for a deeper understanding of the petroglyphs.

Honanki Heritage Site

Historical Significance: Honanki, meaning "Bear House" in Hopi, offers a glimpse into the Sinagua people's way of life. The site includes cliff dwellings and rock art that date back to between 1150 and 1350 CE, showcasing the region's rich archaeological heritage.

Visitor Information:

- **Location**: 1156 Loy Butte Rd, Sedona, AZ 86336
- **Cost**: $10 per vehicle; free with an America the Beautiful Pass.
- **Hours**: Open daily; guided tours available via Pink Jeep Tours.
- **Tips**: A high-clearance vehicle is recommended for access. Combine this visit with Palatki for a comprehensive archaeological experience.

Exploring Sedona's historical and cultural landmarks provides a deep appreciation for the area's ancient and modern significance. Each site offers unique stories, stunning landscapes, and opportunities for reflection, making Sedona a destination where history, spirituality, and natural beauty converge.

Chapter 13: Festivals and Events in Sedona

Sedona is a vibrant hub for cultural celebrations, artistic showcases, and live music events, offering a dynamic calendar of festivals that reflect the city's creative spirit. Having attended many of these festivals myself, I can attest to their magic and the sense of community they inspire. Here's an in-depth guide to Sedona's top events, with practical tips to help you plan your trip to coincide with them.

Art Fairs, Music Festivals, and Cultural Celebrations

Why Go: The Sedona International Film Festival is a must-attend for cinephiles, offering a week-long celebration of independent films, documentaries, and shorts. This festival showcases the works of emerging and seasoned filmmakers, often accompanied by Q&A sessions, workshops, and panel discussions. The intimate atmosphere allows you to engage directly with creators and immerse yourself in the art of filmmaking.
When: Late February (exact dates vary; typically runs for 9 days).
Where: Sedona Performing Arts Center and other venues across the city.
Cost: Individual tickets range from $15–$20 per film. Festival passes start at $250 for a basic pass and go up to $1,200 for all-access VIP experiences.
Planning Tips: Book your festival pass early, as they often sell out quickly. Accommodations in Sedona fill up during this time, so reserve your stay at least two months in advance. Pair the festival with a scenic drive through Sedona's iconic red rocks for a memorable trip.

Sedona Arts Festival

Why Go: This two-day festival in October is an artistic feast, featuring over 100 juried artists showcasing their work across various mediums, including painting, sculpture, ceramics, and jewelry. The event also includes live music, food trucks, and a kid-friendly creative zone, making it perfect for families and art enthusiasts.
When: Mid-October (usually the second or third weekend).
Where: Sedona Red Rock High School.
Cost: $15 for adults; children under 12 enter free. Proceeds support arts education programs in the community.
Planning Tips: Bring cash for purchasing art directly from the artists and sampling food. Arrive early to avoid crowds and enjoy cooler morning temperatures.

Sedona Yoga Festival

Why Go: A transformative experience for mind, body, and spirit, the Sedona Yoga Festival attracts yogis and wellness enthusiasts from around the globe. Held amidst the serene red rock landscapes, this multi-day event features yoga classes, meditation workshops, sound healing sessions, and keynote speakers.
When: March (specific dates vary).
Where: Various venues across Sedona, with outdoor sessions often hosted in scenic locations.
Cost: Passes range from $250–$800, depending on the access level. Single-day passes are also available for around $100.
Planning Tips: Pack comfortable clothing and a good yoga mat. If you're a beginner, look for sessions marked as "all levels." Extend your stay to explore Sedona's vortex sites for a holistic spiritual journey.

Red Rocktoberfest

Why Go: This lively October celebration combines Sedona's love for craft beverages with live music and local food. Hosted in Uptown Sedona, the festival features craft beer tastings, wine, cider, and delicious food options, along with performances by local bands.
When: Early October.
Where: Posse Grounds Park.
Cost: Entry is usually free; tasting tickets cost around $25–$50, depending on the number of samples included.
Planning Tips: Come with an appetite and plan to use rideshares or shuttles if you're sampling alcoholic beverages. The weather is typically mild in October, so outdoor seating is comfortable.

Illuminate Film Festival

Why Go: A unique addition to Sedona's cultural calendar, this festival focuses on transformational films that inspire social change, spiritual growth, and personal transformation. With film screenings, immersive workshops, and discussions with thought leaders, the Illuminate Film Festival provides a deeper cinematic experience.
When: Late May to early June.
Where: Sedona Performing Arts Center and other venues.
Cost: Ticket prices range from $10–$20 per screening. Festival passes start at $200.
Planning Tips: Schedule your trip to include a visit to nearby vortex sites, as many festival attendees find the combination of Sedona's energy and the festival's themes particularly uplifting.

Sedona Music Festival

Why Go: Set against the backdrop of Sedona's stunning landscapes, this annual festival features live performances by regional and national musicians across various genres. From classical ensembles to folk and rock bands, the Sedona Music Festival has something for every music lover.
When: Late spring (exact dates vary).
Where: Posse Grounds Amphitheater and other outdoor venues.
Cost: Tickets range from $25–$75, depending on the performance and seating.
Planning Tips: Bring a blanket or low-back chairs for outdoor seating. Dress in layers to stay comfortable as temperatures drop after sunset.

How to Plan Your Trip

1. **Align Your Dates**: Research the exact dates of your chosen festival and plan your travel around them. Sedona's events often coincide with peak tourist seasons, so advance planning is crucial.
2. **Book Early**: Secure accommodations and tickets as soon as possible, especially for larger events like the Sedona International Film Festival.
3. **Transportation**: Consider renting a car for easier access to multiple venues, especially for festivals like the Sedona Yoga Festival, which uses various locations.
4. **Pack Accordingly**: Depending on the season, pack comfortable walking shoes, sun protection, and layers for cooler evenings.
5. **Extend Your Stay**: Add a day or two to explore Sedona's iconic landmarks, hiking trails, and vortex sites.

Attending Sedona's festivals and events adds a vibrant layer to your visit, blending artistic, cultural, and spiritual experiences that are uniquely Sedona.

Culinary Adventures

Chapter 14: Local Cuisine and Dining Scene

Sedona's dining scene offers a delightful fusion of flavors inspired by the Southwest's rich culinary traditions, fresh local ingredients, and global influences. Whether you're a foodie or simply looking for a memorable meal, the town boasts an impressive selection of restaurants and cafes that cater to a variety of tastes. Having explored Sedona's culinary landscape on multiple visits, here are some of the top dining spots and regional dishes you absolutely shouldn't miss.

Top Restaurants and Cafes

The Hudson

Address: 671 AZ-179 Suite D, Sedona, AZ 86336
Why Go: Perched with stunning views of the red rocks, The Hudson is a modern eatery with a laid-back atmosphere and a menu that highlights hearty, flavorful dishes. Standout offerings include their pork osso buco ($34), shrimp scampi ($26), and the famous Hudson Burger ($20), which pairs perfectly with a local craft beer or a glass of wine. The outdoor patio is ideal for dining at sunset, with the golden light casting dramatic shadows on the rocks.
Cost: Expect to spend $20–$40 per person, excluding drinks.
Tips: Reservations are highly recommended, especially for dinner. Ask for a patio seat to maximize the view.

Elote Café

Address: 350 Jordan Road, Sedona, AZ 86336
Why Go: Elote Café is a Sedona institution, renowned for its elevated take on Mexican and Southwestern cuisine. The elote appetizer ($14) is legendary – roasted corn with a creamy, tangy sauce that sets the tone for an exceptional meal. Other highlights include the lamb adobo ($36) and smoked pork cheeks ($28). The restaurant's use of bold flavors and locally sourced ingredients makes it a must-visit for food lovers.
Cost: Dishes range from $14–$40.
Tips: Arrive early as the restaurant doesn't take reservations, and it gets busy quickly. The bar area is a great spot for solo diners or couples.

Mariposa Latin Inspired Grill

Address: 700 AZ-89A, Sedona, AZ 86336
Why Go: For an upscale dining experience, Mariposa offers a fusion of South American and Latin flavors in an architecturally stunning building with panoramic red rock views. Signature dishes include the wood-fired steaks (starting at $42), fresh ceviche ($18), and empanadas ($16). The handcrafted cocktails, such as the jalapeño margarita, add a refreshing kick to the meal.
Cost: Dinner averages $50–$75 per person.
Tips: This is a great spot for special occasions. Request a table near the window or on the outdoor patio for the best views.

ChocolaTree Organic Eatery

Address: 1595 AZ-89A, Sedona, AZ 86336

Why Go: For health-conscious travelers or those seeking plant-based options, ChocolaTree offers a haven of organic, gluten-free, and vegan-friendly dishes. The cacao chili ($12) and the blissful burger ($14) are packed with flavor and nutrients. Don't miss their handmade raw chocolates and refreshing herbal teas. The tranquil garden seating area makes dining here a serene experience.

Cost: Meals typically cost $10–$20 per person.

Tips: This is a great lunch spot after a morning hike. Grab some chocolates to take home as a delicious souvenir.

Tamaliza

Address: 1155 W SR-89A Suite 124, Sedona, AZ 86336

Why Go: Tamaliza specializes in authentic tamales crafted with organic, non-GMO corn. The red chili pork tamale ($10) and vegetarian green chili tamale ($9) are bursting with traditional flavors. The homemade salsas are the perfect accompaniment, and the casual, colorful setting makes it a great spot for a quick, satisfying meal.

Cost: Most meals are under $15.

Tips: Tamales travel well, so consider ordering extra for a picnic or next-day snack.

Cress on Oak Creek

Address: 301 L'Auberge Lane, Sedona, AZ 86336

Why Go: Set along the serene banks of Oak Creek, Cress offers a fine dining experience with a focus on locally sourced ingredients. The prix-fixe menu ($125 per person) features dishes like seared scallops, elk tenderloin, and decadent chocolate desserts. The tranquil creekside setting enhances the experience, making it ideal for romantic evenings or special celebrations.

Cost: $125 per person for the prix-fixe menu.

Tips: Dress smart-casual and reserve a table well in advance. The outdoor seating by the creek is particularly enchanting.

Sedona's culinary scene is as diverse as its stunning landscapes. Whether you're indulging in fine dining, grabbing a casual bite, or exploring local flavors, the town offers unforgettable experiences for every palate and budget.

Regional Dishes You Can't Miss

Sedona's culinary identity is deeply rooted in the flavors of the Southwest, with an emphasis on fresh, local ingredients and traditional techniques. Each dish tells a story of the region's culture and natural abundance, making dining in Sedona as much about discovery as it is about nourishment. Here's a deeper dive into some must-try regional specialties:

Elote

Elote, or Mexican street corn, is elevated to new heights at the renowned **Elote Café**. This dish features perfectly roasted corn smothered in a rich, creamy sauce made with mayonnaise, cotija cheese, lime, and a hint of smoky chili powder. The combination of sweet, tangy, and spicy flavors makes it a crowd favorite. It's served as an appetizer but is hearty enough to leave a lasting impression.

Where to Try: Elote Café, 350 Jordan Road, Sedona, AZ

Cost: $14

Why It's Special: The smoky sweetness of the grilled corn paired with the bold flavors of the sauce creates a harmony that's both comforting and exciting. This is a dish that celebrates the simplicity of great ingredients.

Southwestern Tamales

At **Tamaliza**, tamales are more than just a meal—they're a work of art. These hand-rolled delights are made with organic, non-GMO corn masa and wrapped in corn husks before being steamed to perfection. Popular varieties include the red chili pork tamale, which is savory and mildly spicy, and the green chili and cheese tamale, a vegetarian favorite bursting with flavor. Each tamale comes with a side of salsa that adds an extra layer of zest.
   Where to Try: Tamaliza, 1155 W SR-89A Suite 124, Sedona, AZ
   Cost: $9–$10 per tamale
   Why It's Special: Tamales are a staple of Southwestern cuisine, and Tamaliza's dedication to authenticity and quality makes theirs some of the best. The combination of earthy masa and flavorful fillings transports you to the heart of the Southwest.

Prickly Pear Margarita

Sedona's signature cocktail, the prickly pear margarita, is a refreshing and vibrant drink that perfectly encapsulates the spirit of the desert. The key ingredient is prickly pear syrup, made from the fruit of the native prickly pear cactus. Its naturally bright magenta hue and sweet, slightly tangy flavor make this drink as beautiful as it is delicious. Paired with tequila, lime juice, and a salted rim, it's the perfect accompaniment to a sunset view.
   Where to Try: Available at numerous Sedona restaurants, including The Hudson and Mariposa Latin Inspired Grill
   Cost: $10–$15
   Why It's Special: Beyond its unique flavor, this cocktail connects you to Sedona's desert landscape in a tangible way. It's like drinking the essence of the region.

Cactus Fries

Cactus fries offer a playful twist on a classic appetizer, using thinly sliced pads of the prickly pear cactus (nopales). These slices are battered, fried until crispy, and served with a tangy dipping sauce like chipotle ranch. The cactus has a slightly tart, green flavor reminiscent of okra, which pairs beautifully with the crunchy coating and creamy dip.
   Where to Try: Cowboy Club Grille & Spirits, 241 N SR-89A, Sedona, AZ
   Cost: $12–$14
   Why It's Special: Cactus fries are a fun and unexpected way to experience the edible bounty of the desert. They're perfect for sharing and make a great starter before diving into a Southwestern feast.

Navajo Tacos

These hearty tacos are served on fry bread—a traditional Native American flatbread that's crispy on the outside and fluffy inside. Toppings include ground beef, beans, lettuce, cheese, and salsa, making them a satisfying meal on their own.
   Where to Try: Sedona Memories Bakery Café, 2081 W SR-89A, Sedona, AZ
   Cost: $10–$12
   Why It's Special: Navajo tacos connect diners to the indigenous roots of the Southwest, offering a unique blend of history and flavor.

Hatch Green Chili Stew

This warming dish features tender chunks of pork simmered with roasted Hatch green chilies, potatoes, and spices. It's a bowl of comfort with a kick of heat, perfect for chilly dessert evenings.
  Where to Try: Mesa Grill, 1185 Airport Road, Sedona, AZ
  Cost: $14–$16
  Why It's Special: Hatch chilies are a staple of Southwestern cooking, and this stew showcases their smoky, spicy depth of flavor in a way that's both traditional and satisfying.

Sedona's culinary adventures are as vibrant and diverse as its landscapes. From the creamy richness of elote to the tart tang of prickly pear margaritas, every bite offers a connection to the region's history, culture, and natural beauty. Dining in Sedona isn't just a meal—it's an essential part of experiencing this magical destination.

Chapter 15: Farm-to-Table and Organic Dining

Sedona is a haven for farm-to-table dining, where local chefs collaborate with farmers and ranchers to create dishes that are as fresh as the surrounding landscapes. The focus on sustainability and organic ingredients ensures every bite is both flavorful and responsibly sourced, making Sedona an ideal destination for conscious foodies.

Supporting Local Farmers and Sustainable Practices

One of the best places to experience Sedona's commitment to local sourcing is **The ChocolaTree Organic Eatery**. This quaint spot offers a fully organic, plant-based menu that caters to various dietary preferences. From hearty quinoa bowls to decadent raw cacao desserts, every dish is made from scratch with ingredients sourced from nearby farms or the restaurant's own garden. The peaceful outdoor patio, shaded by lush greenery, is perfect for enjoying their nourishing creations.

- **Where to Visit**: ChocolaTree Organic Eatery, 1595 W SR-89A, Sedona, AZ
- **Cost**: Entrées range from $12–$18
- **Why It's Special**: This is more than a meal; it's a philosophy. The dedication to sustainability and health shines through in both the food and the serene ambiance.

For those craving upscale dining with a farm-to-table twist, **Mariposa Latin Inspired Grill** offers an unforgettable experience. Perched on a hillside, this restaurant combines stunning views with dishes like wood-fired steak and fresh seafood, complemented by locally sourced vegetables.

- **Where to Visit**: Mariposa Latin Inspired Grill, 700 AZ-89A, Sedona, AZ
- **Cost**: Entrées range from $28–$50
- **Why It's Special**: The restaurant's commitment to quality ingredients and its breathtaking location make every meal a celebration of Sedona's natural bounty.

Food Tours and Unique Experiences

Tasting Tours, Cooking Classes, and More

Exploring Sedona's culinary landscape goes beyond traditional dining. Food tours and cooking classes offer interactive and immersive ways to savor the region's unique flavors.

Sedona Food Tours

A guided food tour is one of the best ways to sample a variety of Sedona's top culinary offerings in a single afternoon. **A Taste of Sedona** food tours combine history, culture, and cuisine as they take participants to local eateries, wineries, and hidden gems. Expect to try dishes like prickly pear-infused appetizers, artisan chocolates, and locally made wines.

- **Cost**: $125–$150 per person (includes food and drinks at each stop)
- **Duration**: 3–4 hours
- **Why It's Special**: The knowledgeable guides provide fascinating insights into Sedona's culinary and cultural history, making this an educational as well as delicious adventure.

Cooking Classes

Learn to prepare Southwestern classics with a hands-on cooking class at **Sedona Culinary School**. Participants are guided by expert chefs who teach techniques for creating dishes like tamales, green chili stew, or desserts using prickly pear syrup. Classes are designed for all skill levels and often conclude with a shared meal.

- **Where to Visit**: Sedona Culinary School, 7000 AZ-179, Sedona, AZ
- **Cost**: $75–$120 per class
- **Why It's Special**: The classes emphasize using fresh, local ingredients, allowing you to bring a piece of Sedona's culinary heritage home with you.

Wine and Dine Experiences

For wine lovers, Sedona's proximity to the Verde Valley Wine Trail opens up opportunities to pair farm-to-table dishes with exceptional local wines. Many tours, such as those offered by **Sedona Vineyard Tours**, include stops at wineries where you can savor everything from crisp whites to robust reds alongside cheese platters and charcuterie boards.

- **Cost**: $125–$180 per person
- **Why It's Special**: This is a chance to explore Sedona's lesser-known wine culture while enjoying the natural beauty of nearby vineyards.

Sedona's farm-to-table movement and culinary experiences offer more than just great food—they provide a deeper connection to the land and its people. Whether dining on organic cuisine, exploring local food tours, or learning new cooking techniques, each adventure celebrates the unique flavors and sustainable practices of this enchanting desert region.

Practical Guide

Chapter 16: Sustainable and Responsible Travel

Visiting Sedona is an opportunity to embrace the region's beauty and culture while contributing positively to its preservation. As a destination renowned for its stunning red rock landscapes and spiritual energy, Sedona requires a mindful approach to tourism. Here's how you can minimize your environmental impact and respect the area's culture and environment.

Tips for Minimizing Your Environmental Impact

1. **Stick to Designated Trails**
   Sedona's trails are meticulously maintained to protect the fragile desert ecosystem. Straying off marked paths can damage plants, disturb wildlife, and lead to soil erosion. Use established trails like Cathedral Rock or Bell Rock to enjoy the scenery responsibly.

   - **Pro Tip**: Use trail apps like AllTrails to ensure you stay on course.

2. **Carry Reusable Gear**
   Single-use plastics are a major environmental concern, even in Sedona's pristine surroundings. Invest in a reusable water bottle, utensils, and shopping bags. Sedona's tap water is safe to drink, and many trailheads have refill stations.

   - **Recommended Gear**: Insulated water bottles ($15–$25) and lightweight bamboo utensils ($10–$15).

3. **Follow Leave No Trace Principles**
   The "Leave No Trace" ethic is essential in Sedona's wilderness. This includes packing out all trash, avoiding graffiti or carving into rocks, and minimizing noise pollution. These practices help preserve Sedona for future generations.

   - **Fun Fact**: Even biodegradable items like fruit peels can disrupt the ecosystem. Always pack them out!

4. **Use Eco-Friendly Transportation**
   Reduce your carbon footprint by opting for Sedona's free **Sedona Shuttle** to popular trailheads like Cathedral Rock and Dry Creek. Alternatively, rent an electric bike for a greener way to explore.

   - **Cost**: Sedona Shuttle is free; e-bike rentals start at $25/hour.

5. **Support Sustainable Businesses**
   Many local shops, restaurants, and tour operators prioritize sustainability. Look for establishments that use locally sourced ingredients, eco-friendly materials, or renewable energy.

   - **Examples**: ChocolaTree Organic Eatery and El Portal Sedona Hotel.

How to Respect Sedona's Culture and Environment

1. **Honor Native American Heritage**
   Sedona is rich in Native American history and culture. Sites like Palatki Heritage Site and the Honanki Ruins hold spiritual significance. Approach these places with reverence, avoid touching

artifacts, and consider hiring a guide to gain deeper insight into their cultural importance.

- - - **Pro Tip**: Visit the **Museum of Northern Arizona** in Flagstaff for an enriching overview of the region's Indigenous history before exploring.
2. **Engage in Low-Impact Spiritual Practices**
Sedona's vortex sites, such as Airport Mesa and Bell Rock, are known for their spiritual energy. If engaging in meditation or ceremonies, keep them private and quiet to avoid disturbing others. Always clean up any offerings or materials used.

3. **Respect Wildlife**
From mule deer to coyotes, Sedona's diverse wildlife is a treasure. Keep your distance, never feed animals, and secure food in your vehicle while hiking. Feeding wildlife can disrupt their natural behaviors and pose risks to both animals and humans.

4. **Limit Noise Pollution**
Many visitors come to Sedona for tranquility and spiritual renewal. Whether hiking, camping, or driving, keep noise levels low to preserve the serene atmosphere for everyone.

5. **Attend Educational Workshops**
Organizations like the **Red Rock Ranger District** offer workshops and events on Sedona's ecology and history. These programs provide invaluable insights into the area's conservation needs and cultural heritage.

    - **Cost**: Free to $10 donation recommended.
6. **Be Mindful of Water Usage**
Sedona's desert climate means water is a precious resource. Use it sparingly, whether at your accommodation or while camping. Many hotels, like **Enchantment Resort**, have adopted water-saving measures—supporting these businesses can make a big difference.

Traveling responsibly in Sedona is about more than minimizing your environmental impact; it's about showing gratitude for the land and its people. By adopting these sustainable practices, you can ensure that your visit leaves a positive legacy in this breathtaking region.

Chapter 17: Safety and Etiquette

Exploring Sedona's vibrant landscapes and cultural landmarks is an incredible experience, but it comes with responsibilities. To ensure your visit is enjoyable, safe, and respectful, it's essential to be aware of trail safety guidelines, emergency protocols, local customs, and proper etiquette.

Trail Safety and Emergency Contacts

1. **Know Your Limits**
   Sedona offers trails for all skill levels, from the leisurely Bell Rock Pathway to the more challenging Cathedral Rock climb. Choose trails that match your fitness level, and avoid attempting strenuous hikes during extreme heat or late in the day.

   - **Pro Tip**: Research trail difficulty on apps like AllTrails before setting out.

2. **Hydration and Sun Protection**
   The desert sun can be harsh, even in cooler months. Always carry at least **1 liter of water per hour of hiking**, wear sunscreen (SPF 30 or higher), and bring a wide-brimmed hat and sunglasses.

   - **Tip**: Electrolyte packets can help replenish minerals lost through sweat.

3. **Prepare for Emergencies**
   Cell service is unreliable in many parts of Sedona. Carry a **paper map**, a charged GPS device, and a basic first aid kit. Inform someone of your itinerary and expected return time.

   - **Emergency Contacts**: Dial **911** for life-threatening situations. For non-emergencies, contact the **Red Rock Ranger District Office** at (928) 203-2900.

4. **Watch for Wildlife and Hazards**
   Be aware of rattlesnakes, scorpions, and other desert creatures. Stay on designated trails to avoid hidden hazards like loose rocks and cactus spines.

   - **Wildlife Tip**: If you encounter a snake, back away slowly; never attempt to handle or provoke it.

5. **Hiking During Monsoon Season**
   From late June to early September, sudden storms can cause dangerous flash flooding in dry washes. Check weather forecasts before heading out and avoid hiking in areas prone to flooding.

   - **Resource**: Monitor local weather updates via the **National Weather Service Flagstaff**.

6. **Trail Etiquette**

   - Yield to uphill hikers.
   - Keep noise levels low to preserve the peaceful ambiance.
   - Pack out all trash, including biodegradable items.

Local Customs and Dos and Don'ts

1. **Respect Sacred Sites**
   Sedona is home to many Native American heritage sites and vortexes considered sacred by Indigenous cultures. Do not climb, deface, or leave items at these locations unless guided by

cultural traditions.

- ○ **Example**: The Chapel of the Holy Cross is both a historical and spiritual site—maintain silence and refrain from disruptive behavior during your visit.

2. **Photography Etiquette**
Sedona's beauty is a photographer's dream, but always ask permission before photographing locals or private properties. At sacred sites, be mindful of rules prohibiting photography.

3. **Leave No Trace**
Follow the "Leave No Trace" principles by packing out all waste, staying on trails, and avoiding damage to flora and fauna. Sedona's unique environment is fragile and requires care.

4. **Interact with Locals Politely**
The residents of Sedona take pride in their community. If you need directions or recommendations, approach locals respectfully and thank them for their help.

5. **Mind Parking Rules**
Popular trailheads often have limited parking. Use the **Sedona Shuttle** or carpool to reduce congestion. Parking illegally on residential streets can result in fines.

- ○ **Tip**: Arrive early to secure a spot or plan to hike during off-peak hours.

6. **Support Local Businesses**
From farm-to-table restaurants to artisan shops, Sedona thrives on its local economy. Prioritize spending at small businesses and tip generously when dining out (15–20% is standard in the U.S.).

7. **Avoid Over-Tourism Practices**
Sedona can become overcrowded during peak seasons. If you notice a trail or site is congested, consider exploring lesser-known areas to reduce strain on popular spots.

8. **Cultural Sensitivity**
Many locals and visitors practice spiritual ceremonies at Sedona's vortexes. Be respectful by keeping noise levels low and observing from a distance.

By following these safety tips and respecting local customs, you can enjoy Sedona's breathtaking landscapes and rich culture while ensuring that the region remains a welcoming and unspoiled destination for future visitors.

Chapter 18: Planning Resources

Sample Itineraries

Sedona offers a variety of experiences, whether you're visiting for just one day, a weekend, or an entire week. Below are three sample itineraries designed to help you make the most of your time in this captivating region. Each itinerary is packed with must-see spots, local activities, and highlights tailored to different durations of stay.

One-Day Highlights

Morning:

- **8:00 AM - Cathedral Rock**: Start your day with a sunrise hike at Cathedral Rock. This iconic landmark offers breathtaking views over Sedona's red rock formations. The trail is moderately challenging, taking about 1-2 hours round-trip.
- **10:30 AM - Breakfast at Sedona's Favorite Café**: Head back to town for a hearty breakfast at a local café like **Pisa Lisa** or **Creekside American Bistro**. Try Southwestern specialties like huevos rancheros or breakfast burritos.
- **12:00 PM - Chapel of the Holy Cross**: Visit this architectural marvel that blends into the red rock landscape. The spiritual energy here is palpable, and the views are spectacular. Spend about 30 minutes here to soak in the serene environment.
- **1:30 PM - Lunchtime at Tlaquepaque Arts and Shopping Village**: For lunch, explore the charming Tlaquepaque Arts and Shopping Village. Try the farm-to-table offerings at **Mariposa Latin Inspired Grill**. The village's cobbled streets are also great for a leisurely stroll and some shopping.
- **3:00 PM - Devil's Bridge Jeep Tour**: Embark on a guided jeep tour to Devil's Bridge, one of Sedona's most famous natural landmarks. The tour offers not only incredible views but also fascinating local stories. The drive takes around 3-4 hours in total.
- **6:00 PM - Dinner at Elote Café**: Wrap up your day with dinner at **Elote Café**, famous for its inventive Southwestern dishes like the creamy Elote (corn dish) and prickly pear margaritas. The vibrant atmosphere and mouth watering menu make it a perfect ending to your day.

Cost Estimate:

- **Cathedral Rock Hike**: Free
- **Breakfast**: $10–15 per person
- **Chapel of the Holy Cross**: Free, but donations are encouraged
- **Lunch**: $15–20 per person
- **Jeep Tour**: $150–200 per person
- **Dinner**: $25–35 per person

Three-Day Adventure

Day 1:

- **Morning**: Begin your adventure with a visit to **Bell Rock** and **Courthouse Butte Loop Trail**. This is a great intro to Sedona's landscape with stunning views and a moderate hike that takes about 2-3 hours.

- **Afternoon**: After a morning of hiking, relax with a lunch at **Tlaquepaque Arts and Shopping Village** and explore its shops, galleries, and eateries. Spend the afternoon discovering local art galleries and the Sedona Arts Center.
- **Evening**: Conclude your day with a guided vortex tour. The energy at **Airport Mesa** is strong and the sunset views are spectacular. It's a peaceful, reflective way to end your day.

Day 2:

- **Morning**: Head to **Red Rock Crossing** and Crescent Moon Picnic Site for an easy hike along Oak Creek. These areas are perfect for photography, picnicking, and enjoying the natural beauty of the area.
- **Afternoon**: After lunch, visit **Slide Rock State Park** to cool off in the natural water slides or just enjoy a peaceful afternoon by the creek. The park's rustic setting is ideal for both adventure and relaxation.
- **Evening**: Attend the **Sedona International Film Festival** if it coincides with your visit, or explore local dining options. Try **Tii Gavo**, a local favorite known for its stunning views and delicious southwestern cuisine.

Day 3:

- **Morning**: Get an early start with a hike on **Bear Mountain** for panoramic views of Sedona. This challenging trail is best for those looking for a more strenuous morning activity.
- **Afternoon**: Spend the day exploring **Palatki Heritage Site** to learn about Sedona's history and indigenous rock art. The site offers guided tours that make the history come alive.
- **Evening**: Return to town for a relaxing dinner at **Mariposa Latin Inspired Grill** at Tlaquepaque Arts and Shopping Village, followed by a visit to the **Sedona Arts Center** to experience local artists at work.

Cost Estimate:

- **Bell Rock Hike**: Free
- **Tlaquepaque Village**: Free to wander, but dining costs range from $10–30 per person
- **Vortex Tour**: $25–50 per person
- **Red Rock Crossing**: Free
- **Slide Rock State Park**: $20 per vehicle
- **Bear Mountain Hike**: Free
- **Palatki Heritage Site**: $12 per person for a guided tour
- **Dinner**: $20–30 per person

Week-Long Immersion

Day 1-2:

- **Day 1**: Arrive in Sedona and settle into your accommodations. Spend the morning hiking **Cathedral Rock** and the afternoon exploring **Tlaquepaque Arts and Shopping Village**.
- **Day 2**: Hike **Bell Rock** and Courthouse Butte Loop Trail in the morning, then visit **Chapel of the Holy Cross** and take a vortex tour at Airport Mesa in the afternoon.

Day 3-4:

- **Day 3**: Head out early for a jeep tour to **Devil's Bridge**, then spend the afternoon hiking **Red Rock Crossing** and enjoying a quiet evening with a picnic at **Crescent Moon Picnic Site**.
- **Day 4**: Visit **Slide Rock State Park** and **Palatki Heritage Site** for a deep dive into Sedona's natural beauty and history. Wrap up the day with a local dinner at **Elote Café**.

Day 5-6:

- **Day 5**: Explore the **Oak Creek Canyon and Slide Rock State Park** for hiking and swimming. Spend the afternoon visiting **Sedona's art galleries** and attending a local craft fair.
- **Day 6**: Take a full day trip to **Bear Mountain** for an intense hike and then relax with a late afternoon visit to **Tlaquepaque Arts and Shopping Village** for dinner and shopping.

Day 7:

- **Morning**: Head out for a final easy hike at **Airport Mesa** or **Sunset Crater** to soak in the views.
- **Afternoon**: Spend your last hours in Sedona exploring **Historical and Cultural Landmarks** such as the **Chapel of the Holy Cross** and **Palatki Heritage Site**.
- **Evening**: Wrap up your trip with a visit to **Mariposa Latin Inspired Grill** at Tlaquepaque Arts and Shopping Village for dinner, enjoying your final sunset views over Sedona.

Cost Estimate:

- **Cathedral Rock Hike**: Free
- **Tlaquepaque Village**: Free to wander, but dining costs range from $15–30 per person
- **Vortex Tour**: $25–50 per person
- **Devil's Bridge Jeep Tour**: $150–200 per person
- **Red Rock Crossing**: Free
- **Slide Rock State Park**: $20 per vehicle
- **Palatki Heritage Site**: $12 per person for a guided tour
- **Bear Mountain Hike**: Free
- **Dinner at Tlaquepaque**: $20–30 per person
- **Mariposa**: $25–35 per person

These itineraries provide a balanced mix of adventure, relaxation, and cultural exploration, ensuring that you experience the best of Sedona no matter your length of stay.

Sedona for Families

Sedona is a family-friendly destination offering a mix of outdoor adventures, kid-friendly activities, and comfortable accommodations. Whether you're planning a short weekend getaway or a longer stay, here's a guide to help you make the most of your family vacation in Sedona.

Kid-Friendly Activities and Trails

Outdoor Adventures:

1. **Red Rock Crossing**: This area is perfect for families. The gentle creek here is shallow and safe for children to splash around in, making it a great spot for a family picnic or just enjoying the

natural beauty. The walk to the creek is short and accessible for all ages.

- **Distance**: 0.5 miles round-trip from the parking area to the creek.
- **Cost**: Free
2. **Slide Rock State Park**: A popular destination for families, this park offers natural water slides formed by the river over smooth red rock. It's a fantastic place for kids to play safely in the water, especially on hot summer days.

    - **Cost**: $20 per vehicle for day use.
    - **Hours**: 8:00 AM - 6:00 PM during the warmer months.
    - **Safety Tip**: Life jackets are recommended for young children, especially on the water slides.
3. **Hiking Trails**:

    - **Little Horse Trail to Chicken Point**: This is an easy to moderate hike that offers stunning views of the red rock formations. The trail is suitable for kids, taking about 2-3 hours round-trip. The wide, well-marked path makes it manageable for families.
        - **Distance**: 3 miles round-trip.
        - **Cost**: Free
    - **Airport Loop Trail**: This short, family-friendly trail offers beautiful scenery and educational markers about the local environment. The loop is about 2 miles long and is mostly flat, making it great for kids.
        - **Distance**: 2 miles round-trip.
        - **Cost**: Free
4. **Tlaquepaque Arts and Shopping Village**: A charming outdoor shopping area perfect for families. The village is full of art galleries, boutiques, and places to stop for ice cream or a quick snack. It's also a great place for kids to practice their photography.

    - **Cost**: Free to wander; costs for food vary.
    - **Hours**: Open daily, with many shops opening around 10 AM.
5. **Wildlife Viewing**: The Sedona Wetlands Preserve is a beautiful place to observe local wildlife in a family-friendly environment. With walking trails and observation decks, it's a peaceful spot for kids to learn about nature.

    - **Cost**: Free
    - **Hours**: Sunrise to sunset.

Indoor Activities:

- **Sedona Children's Museum**: Located at the Hillside Sedona complex, this museum offers a range of interactive exhibits that are both educational and entertaining for children. It's a great place to escape the heat or bad weather.

    - **Cost**: $5 per person.
    - **Hours**: 10 AM - 4 PM.

- **Red Rock Magic Trolley**: A fun and informative trolley tour for families. It's a great way to learn about Sedona's history and geology while seeing the sights from a comfortable trolley.

    - **Cost**: $25 per adult, $10 per child.
    - **Duration**: About 1.5 hours.
    - **Hours**: Several tours available daily from March to October.
- **Outdoor Family Adventures**:

    - **Hot Air Balloon Rides**: Although not specifically kid-friendly due to age restrictions, older children (around 5 years and older) can enjoy a magical balloon ride over Sedona's red rock country.
        - **Cost**: Around $200 per person.
        - **Hours**: Early morning flights.

Best Family Accommodations

Hotels:

1. **Hilton Sedona Resort at Bell Rock**:

    - This family-friendly resort offers spacious rooms and a variety of amenities including a large outdoor pool, tennis courts, and a children's activity center.
    - **Cost**: Rates start around $250 per night.
    - **Address**: 90 Ridge Trail Dr, Sedona, AZ 86351.
2. **L'Auberge de Sedona**:

    - Located along Oak Creek, this resort provides a more luxurious experience with kid-friendly options such as family suites and a variety of outdoor activities.
    - **Cost**: Rates start at around $450 per night.
    - **Address**: 301 L'Auberge Ln, Sedona, AZ 86336.
3. **Hilton Sedona Resort at Slide Rock**:

    - Situated near Slide Rock State Park, this hotel is great for families looking to be close to outdoor activities. The hotel offers family suites and a kids' program.
    - **Cost**: Rates start at $200 per night.
    - **Address**: 301 Lone Tree Rd, Sedona, AZ 86336.

Vacation Rentals:

- **Airbnb and VRBO**: Sedona has many vacation rental options that are great for families. Many properties offer amenities like kitchens, private pools, and multiple bedrooms, which are perfect for families.
    - **Cost**: Ranges from $100 to $500 per night, depending on size and location.
    - **Example**: A 3-bedroom home near Red Rock Crossing can cost around $300 per night.
    - **Address**: Varies by property.

Camping:

- **National Forest Campgrounds**: For families looking to experience the great outdoors, there are several campgrounds around Sedona, such as **Coconino National Forest Campgrounds**.
    - **Cost**: $20–30 per night for a basic tent site.
    - **Reservations**: Recommended during peak seasons.
    - **Address**: Various campgrounds available around Sedona.

Tips for Booking:

- **Book Early**: Sedona is a popular destination, especially during peak seasons. Booking accommodations and activities well in advance is crucial.
- **Look for Family-Friendly Deals**: Many hotels and resorts offer family packages that include tickets to local attractions, discounts on dining, and other amenities.
- **Check for Kid-Friendly Policies**: Some hotels and vacation rentals provide items like cribs, high chairs, and baby-proofed areas to ensure safety and comfort for families with young children.
- **Consider Proximity**: Choose accommodations based on the family's interests, whether it's proximity to hiking trails, swimming spots, or kid-friendly restaurants.

With these resources, planning a family vacation to Sedona can be a breeze, ensuring a memorable and enjoyable experience for everyone in the family.

Sedona for Couples

Romantic Getaways, Sunset Spots, and Experiences

Sedona is a dreamy destination for couples, offering a perfect blend of natural beauty, adventure, and relaxation. Whether you're celebrating a special occasion, planning a romantic escape, or simply looking for a peaceful retreat, Sedona has something to offer. Here's a guide to help you plan the ultimate romantic getaway in Sedona.

Romantic Getaways

1. Stay at a Cozy Retreat:

- **Amara Resort and Spa**: Located right in the heart of Sedona, this luxurious resort offers stunning views of the red rocks and a tranquil atmosphere. The adult-only policy ensures a peaceful escape from the usual hustle and bustle.
    - **Cost**: Rates start at around $400 per night.
    - **Address**: 100 Amara Ln, Sedona, AZ 86336.
- **L'Auberge de Sedona**: Nestled along Oak Creek, this resort is known for its charming cottages and intimate setting. Each cottage comes with a private deck and whirlpool tub, perfect for a romantic soak under the stars.
    - **Cost**: Rates start at around $500 per night.
    - **Address**: 301 L'Auberge Ln, Sedona, AZ 86336.
- **Sedona Rouge Hotel & Spa**: A bit off the beaten path but still close to the action, this hotel offers luxurious accommodations with views of the red rocks and a top-notch spa for couples to enjoy.
    - **Cost**: Rates start at around $300 per night.
    - **Address**: 2250 W Highway 89A, Sedona, AZ 86336.

2. Private Vacation Rentals:

- For a more secluded experience, consider renting a private cabin or house. Many vacation rentals offer amenities like hot tubs, fireplaces, and fully equipped kitchens, perfect for a romantic evening in.
    - **Example**: A 2-bedroom cabin with a private hot tub can cost around $250 per night.
    - **Address**: Varies by property.
- **Airbnb** and **VRBO** also offer numerous options for couples looking for a romantic setting. Choose a place with a view of the red rocks or one that's nestled in the forest for added privacy.
    - **Cost**: Ranges from $150 to $400 per night, depending on size and location.
    - **Example**: A 1-bedroom cottage with a creek view could cost around $200 per night.
    - **Address**: Varies by property.

Sunset Spots and Experiences

1. Cathedral Rock:

- One of the most iconic spots in Sedona, Cathedral Rock offers breathtaking views at sunset. The hike up to the top is worth it for the panoramic views of the surrounding red rocks and valleys.
    - **Distance**: 1.5 miles round-trip to the base of Cathedral Rock; additional 0.5 miles to the top.
    - **Cost**: Free.
    - **Timing**: The best time to hike is late afternoon to catch the sunset from the summit.
- **Tip**: Arrive early to find a good parking spot and bring a flashlight for the hike down if you stay for the sunset.

2. Red Rock Crossing:

- Another popular spot, especially for couples, Red Rock Crossing is serene and stunning. The view of Cathedral Rock from here is unbeatable, and it's a perfect spot for a picnic or a quiet moment together.
    - **Cost**: Free.
    - **Timing**: Sunset is magical here, but the area can be crowded, so plan to arrive early to get a good spot.
- **Tip**: Bring a picnic blanket and enjoy the serene view with your loved one.

3. Enchantment Resort:

- Located a bit off the main drag, Enchantment Resort is known for its stunning views, luxurious accommodations, and excellent dining options. The resort offers romantic evening programs like guided stargazing and bonfires.
    - **Cost**: Rates start at around $600 per night.
    - **Address**: 525 Boynton Canyon Rd, Sedona, AZ 86336.
- **Tip**: Book a dinner reservation at Tii Gavo for a fine dining experience with views of the red rocks. Their outdoor seating allows you to enjoy a sunset meal while gazing at the beauty of Sedona.

4. Tlaquepaque Arts and Crafts Village:

- This outdoor shopping area is not only beautiful but also perfect for a romantic stroll. The Spanish-style architecture, art galleries, and unique shops make it a romantic evening out.
    - **Cost**: Free to wander; costs for dining and shopping vary.

- **Hours**: Open daily, with shops and galleries opening around 10 AM.
- **Tip**: Plan a late afternoon visit to Tlaquepaque, enjoy a leisurely dinner at one of the excellent restaurants here, and then catch the sunset views from the outdoor patio.

5. Hot Air Balloon Rides:

- For a truly romantic experience, consider a hot air balloon ride over Sedona's red rocks. This is a once-in-a-lifetime experience, offering breathtaking views and a sense of adventure.
    - **Cost**: Around $200 per person.
    - **Hours**: Early morning flights, starting around 6 AM.
- **Tip**: Book a private balloon ride for a more intimate experience. Many balloon companies offer champagne toasts and personalized flights for couples.

Experiences for Couples

1. Couples' Spa Day:

- Sedona is renowned for its healing vortex energy, and what better way to experience it than with a couples' massage? Many of the resorts offer spa services tailored for couples, including hot stone massages, mud wraps, and energy healing sessions.
    - **Cost**: Spa treatments start at around $150 per person for basic services.
    - **Tip**: Book in advance, especially during peak seasons.
    - **Address**: Various spas within resorts like Enchantment Resort and L'Auberge de Sedona.

2. Culinary Delights:

- Sedona has a fantastic food scene, perfect for a romantic date night. From fine dining experiences to cozy, intimate restaurants, there's something for every couple.
    - **Options**:
        - **Rene at Tlaquepaque**: A romantic French restaurant with a serene outdoor patio and a menu that includes classic French dishes.
            - **Cost**: $100 for two with wine.
            - **Address**: 336 SR-179, Sedona, AZ 86336.
        - **Elote Café**: For a more casual vibe, Elote Café offers delicious Southwestern cuisine in a cozy, intimate setting.
            - **Cost**: $50 for two.
            - **Address**: 350 Jordan Rd, Sedona, AZ 86336.

3. Outdoor Adventures:

- Sedona's stunning landscapes provide the perfect backdrop for outdoor adventures for couples. Whether it's a guided Jeep tour through the backcountry, a peaceful horseback ride through the red rocks, or a kayaking trip on Oak Creek, Sedona offers a variety of experiences to bond over nature.
    - **Cost**:
        - **Jeep Tours**: $100–150 per person for a half-day tour.
        - **Horseback Riding**: $60 per person for a 2-hour ride.
    - **Address**: Various outfitters around Sedona.

4. **Stargazing**:

- Sedona's clear skies make it an excellent destination for stargazing. Many resorts and tour companies offer guided stargazing tours with telescopes. You can cuddle up with your loved one under the stars while learning about the constellations.
    - **Cost**: Around $75 per person.
    - **Address**: Various locations throughout Sedona, including the Enchantment Resort and Sky Ranch Lodge.
- **Tip**: Plan a late evening activity after a romantic dinner for a magical conclusion to your day.

With these suggestions, planning a romantic getaway in Sedona can be a breeze. From cozy accommodations to breathtaking sunsets and intimate experiences, Sedona offers everything you need for a memorable escape with your loved one.

Sedona for Solo Travelers

Exploring Sedona on your own can be a deeply rewarding experience, allowing you to connect with its natural beauty, meet like-minded people, and enjoy some much-needed solitude. Whether you're looking for outdoor adventures, cultural experiences, or peaceful retreats, Sedona offers plenty of options for solo travelers. Here's a guide to help you make the most of your solo trip to Sedona.

Safe Adventures

1. **Hiking**:

- **Bell Rock Pathway**: One of the most popular trails in Sedona, Bell Rock Pathway is ideal for solo hikers. The trail offers relatively easy terrain, great views, and minimal elevation gain, making it perfect for all fitness levels.
    - **Distance**: 4.6 miles round-trip.
    - **Cost**: Free.
    - **Address**: Located off State Route 179, south of Sedona.
- **Tip**: Start your hike early in the morning to avoid crowds and to enjoy a peaceful atmosphere. Let someone know your plans before you go.

2. **Cathedral Rock**:

- For more adventurous solo hikers, Cathedral Rock is a challenging yet rewarding trail. The scramble up to the summit offers stunning 360-degree views of the red rock formations.
    - **Distance**: 1.5 miles to the base, with an additional 0.5 miles to the summit.
    - **Cost**: Free.
    - **Address**: Located off Back O' Beyond Rd, near Sedona.
- **Tip**: Bring plenty of water and wear sturdy footwear as the terrain can be rocky and slippery. Start early to avoid the midday sun.

3. **Red Rock Crossing**:

- Another great spot for solo travelers, Red Rock Crossing offers beautiful views of Cathedral Rock. It's a peaceful place to meditate or simply relax.
    - **Cost**: Free.
    - **Address**: Located off Chapel Road, north of Sedona.

- **Tip**: Bring a picnic lunch and make a day of it. Arriving early ensures you get a good spot away from the crowds.

4. **Jeep Tours**:

- For those who want a solo adventure but prefer a guided experience, consider booking a Jeep tour. These tours take you through rugged backcountry and provide an intimate setting with knowledgeable guides.
    - **Cost**: Around $100–150 per person for a half-day tour.
    - **Address**: Various tour operators around Sedona.
- **Tip**: Book a tour in advance to ensure a spot, especially if traveling during peak seasons. The smaller, more personalized tours are ideal for solo travelers.

Social Opportunities

1. **Art Galleries and Studios**:

- Sedona's vibrant art scene offers plenty of opportunities to meet people. Visiting galleries like Hozho Gallery, Tlaquepaque Arts and Crafts Village, and Goldenstein Gallery can provide a cultural and social experience.
    - **Cost**: Free to browse, with prices varying for artwork.
    - **Address**: Various locations around Sedona.
- **Tip**: Attend the free gallery events or artist receptions. They often have light refreshments and are a great way to meet locals and fellow travelers.

2. **Tlaquepaque Arts and Crafts Village**:

- This outdoor shopping area is perfect for solo travelers looking to mingle. The beautiful setting and variety of shops make it a great place to stroll, relax, and meet people.
    - **Cost**: Free to wander; costs for dining and shopping vary.
    - **Hours**: Open daily from around 10 AM to 5 PM.
- **Tip**: Stop for lunch at one of the village's cafes and strike up a conversation with other diners. It's a great way to meet people from around the world.

3. **Local Events and Classes**:

- Check out local events like the Sedona Arts Center's workshops, which cover everything from painting to pottery. These events often attract a friendly crowd of locals and visitors alike.
    - **Cost**: Varies by class, typically around $25–$50.
    - **Address**: Sedona Arts Center, 15 Art Barn Rd, Sedona, AZ 86336.
- **Tip**: Signing up for a class is an excellent way to meet people with similar interests in a relaxed, creative environment.

4. **Dining Alone**:

- Sedona's dining scene is diverse and welcoming to solo diners. Restaurants like The Hudson, Elote Café, and L'Auberge de Sedona are ideal for solo travelers looking to enjoy a good meal and possibly strike up a conversation with locals or other travelers.
    - **Cost**: $20–$50 for a meal.
    - **Addresses**:

- **The Hudson**: 671 SR-179, Sedona, AZ 86336.
- **Elote Café**: 350 Jordan Rd, Sedona, AZ 86336.
- **L'Auberge de Sedona**: 301 L'Auberge Ln, Sedona, AZ 86336.
- **Tip**: Sit at the bar if possible, as bartenders often engage with solo diners, and it's a great way to meet people.

5. **Sunset Spots**:

- Watching the sunset alone can be a deeply personal and moving experience. Places like Airport Mesa and Red Rock Crossing offer incredible views of the sunset over the red rocks.
    - **Cost**: Free.
    - **Timing**: Arrive at least 30 minutes before sunset for a good spot.
- **Tip**: Bring a blanket and a thermos of your favorite drink to make the moment even more special. It's a peaceful and introspective way to end the day.

Sedona for solo travelers is all about finding peace, adventure, and connection. Whether you're hiking in the morning, enjoying a meal at a local café, or meeting people at a gallery event in the evening, there are endless ways to fill your days with meaningful and enriching experiences. Embrace the freedom of solo travel in Sedona and let the beauty and serenity of this magical place enhance your journey.

Chapter 19: Frequently Asked Questions (FAQs)

Common Concerns Addressed

1. **Is Sedona safe for solo travelers?**

    o **Yes, Sedona is generally a safe destination for solo travelers.** The town is known for its friendly atmosphere and low crime rates. However, it's always wise to exercise standard travel precautions like staying aware of your surroundings, avoiding hiking alone at night, and letting someone know your plans when exploring remote areas.

2. **What is the best time to visit Sedona?**

    o **The best time to visit Sedona is from March to May and September to November.** The weather is mild during these months, making outdoor activities more enjoyable. Summer (June to August) can be very hot, while winter (December to February) brings cooler temperatures and occasional snowfall, which can be beautiful but limit some activities.

3. **Do I need a permit to hike in Sedona?**

    o **Most trails in Sedona do not require a special permit, except for a few popular spots like Cathedral Rock and West Fork Oak Creek Trail.** Permits are generally free but must be obtained online or in person at local ranger stations. Check with the Sedona Parks and Recreation website for specific details on permits and requirements.

4. **What should I pack for my trip to Sedona?**

    o **Pack layers for variable weather conditions, sturdy hiking shoes, a wide-brimmed hat, sunscreen, and plenty of water.** A daypack is also essential for carrying water, snacks, a map, and a first aid kit. If visiting during the cooler months, consider packing warm clothing for the evenings.

5. **Are there any cultural or etiquette norms to be aware of in Sedona?**

    o **Yes, respect the local environment and cultural practices.** Do not disturb Native American spiritual sites, pack out all your trash, and avoid leaving offerings at Vortex sites. Tread lightly on hiking trails to minimize erosion and wear appropriate footwear to protect the delicate desert environment.

6. **How do I get around Sedona without a car?**

    o **Sedona is not a large town, but public transportation options are limited.** The Sedona Shuttle service provides transportation within the town, and there are also local taxi services. For more adventurous solo travelers, renting a bike is a great way to explore the area.

7. **What are the must-visit art galleries in Sedona?**

    o **Sedona's art scene is a highlight.** Don't miss Tlaquepaque Arts and Crafts Village, Goldenstein Gallery, and the Hozho Gallery. These galleries showcase local art and provide a unique cultural experience. Most galleries are free to browse, but some may charge for special exhibitions.

8. **Can I find gluten-free or vegan food options in Sedona?**

    - **Yes, Sedona has several restaurants catering to dietary restrictions.** For gluten-free or vegan options, consider visiting restaurants like The Hudson, Wildflower, and Elote Café. These places offer diverse menus that cater to various dietary needs while embracing the local cuisine.

Additional Resources

Websites, Apps, and Local Contacts

1. **Visit Sedona** - www.visitsedona.com

   - **Official visitor's website** with information on events, lodging, dining, and activities.
   - **Features:** Interactive map, trail guides, and calendar of events.

2. **Sedona Chamber of Commerce** - www.sedonachamber.com

   - **Chamber website** offering insights into local businesses, accommodations, and community events.
   - **Features:** Business directory, local news, and visitor resources.

3. **Sedona Hiking** - www.sedonahiking.org

   - **Dedicated hiking website** with trail maps, difficulty ratings, and descriptions.
   - **Features:** Detailed information on over 100 trails in Sedona, including trailheads, distances, and safety tips.

4. **AllTrails - Download the app**

   - **Popular outdoor recreation app** offering trail maps, reviews, and GPS tracking.
   - **Features:** Offline map availability, trail conditions, and user-generated reviews to help you find and navigate Sedona's trails.

5. **Sedona Parks and Recreation - Phone: (928) 282-7098**

   - **Local contact for trail permits and recreational information.**
   - **Features:** Information on park hours, fees, and special permits for popular trails like Cathedral Rock.

6. **National Weather Service Sedona - Phone: (928) 772-0321**

   - **Local weather information** to help you plan outdoor activities.
   - **Features:** Daily weather forecasts, alerts, and advisories for Sedona and the surrounding areas.

7. **Sedona Rouge Hotel & Spa - Address:** 2250 W SR 89A, Sedona, AZ 86336

   - **Contact:** (928) 204-7744
   - **Features:** Full-service hotel with information on tours, dining options, and local activities.
   - **Tip:** The hotel's concierge can assist with booking activities and provide insider tips on exploring Sedona.

These resources will help you plan your trip to Sedona, ensuring you have all the necessary information for a safe, enjoyable, and memorable experience. Whether you're hiking in the red rocks, exploring art galleries, or simply enjoying the local cuisine, Sedona offers something for everyone.

Bonus

Budget Plans

5-Day Budget Plan for Sedona

Day 1: Arrival and Orientation

- **Transportation**: If flying, land at Phoenix Sky Harbor International Airport and take a shuttle to Sedona (Groome Transportation, $60 one-way). Alternatively, rent a car ($50/day for an economy car).
- **Accommodation**: Check into a budget-friendly motel such as **Sedona Motel** (from $90/night).
- **Activities**:
    - Visit **Sedona Visitor Center** (free) for maps and recommendations.
    - Stroll through **Tlaquepaque Arts & Shopping Village** to admire local art and enjoy window shopping (free).
- **Meals**:
    - Breakfast at a casual café en route, like **Wildflower Bread Company** ($10–$12).
    - Lunch at **Sedona Food Truck Park** for affordable eats ($10).
    - Dinner at **Tamaliza Café**, featuring authentic tamales (entrees from $12).
- **Estimated Daily Total**: $182–$214.

Day 2: Exploring Iconic Trails and Natural Wonders

- **Breakfast**: Pick up pastries and coffee at **Sedonuts** ($8).
- **Activities**:
    - Hike **Bell Rock Pathway** for stunning views (free parking at designated lots, or $5/day Red Rock Pass).
    - Visit **Chapel of the Holy Cross** (free; $2 donation suggested).
    - Spend the afternoon at **Red Rock Crossing** for scenic views and photography ($10 per vehicle entry).
- **Lunch**: Pack sandwiches from **New Frontiers Natural Market** ($12).
- **Dinner**: Eat at **Picazzo's Healthy Italian Kitchen** for a hearty, budget-conscious meal (entrees from $15).
- **Estimated Daily Total**: $145–$170.

Day 3: Cultural and Spiritual Exploration

- **Breakfast**: Enjoy a simple meal at **The Coffee Pot Restaurant** ($10).
- **Activities**:
    - Explore **Sedona Heritage Museum** for insight into the region's history ($7 entry fee).
    - Visit a Vortex site, such as **Airport Mesa** (free, $3 parking fee).
    - Browse local galleries like **Exposures International Gallery of Fine Art** (free).
- **Lunch**: Affordable fare at **Sedona Memories Bakery** ($9).
- **Dinner**: Dine at **Hideaway House**, a cozy spot with affordable entrees (from $15).
- **Estimated Daily Total**: $125–$150.

Day 4: Adventure and Outdoor Activities

- **Breakfast**: Stop by **The Local Juicery** for a smoothie and healthy bite ($12).
- **Activities**:
  - Take a budget-friendly **Jeep tour** of Sedona's backcountry with a group rate (approx. $60).
  - Spend the afternoon at **Slide Rock State Park**, enjoying natural water slides ($10 entrance fee).
- **Lunch**: Grab tacos at **Tortas de Fuego** ($10).
- **Dinner**: Enjoy affordable comfort food at **Cowboy Club Grille** (entrees from $17).
- **Estimated Daily Total**: $169–$189.

Day 5: Departure and Last-Minute Sightseeing

- **Breakfast**: Pick up coffee and a bagel at **Starbucks** or a local café ($8).
- **Activities**:
  - Take a quick hike at **Devil's Bridge** for iconic photo ops (free parking with Red Rock Pass, $5 if not already purchased).
  - Drive along **Oak Creek Canyon Scenic Byway** on your way out (free).
- **Lunch**: Eat at **Indian Gardens Café**, a budget-friendly local favorite (entrees from $12).
- **Transportation**: Drive or take a shuttle back to Phoenix for your flight.
- **Estimated Daily Total**: $115–$140.

Total Estimated Cost for 5 Days:

- **Transportation**: $120–$350 (shuttle vs. car rental).
- **Accommodation**: $450.
- **Food**: $220–$260.
- **Activities and Fees**: $100–$130.
- **Total: $890–$1,190.**

This plan offers flexibility while keeping costs low, ensuring you experience Sedona's best without overspending.

3- Day Travel Journal

Pre-Trip Reflections

Date: _____

- What excites me most about this trip?

_____

- What are my top three must-see places?
1. _____
2. _____
3. _____
- How do I feel about this journey?

_____
_____
_____

- Why am I traveling to New England?

_____
_____

- What am I most excited to experience?

_____
_____

- What do I hope to discover or learn?

_____
_____
_____

Day 1: Arrival and First Impressions

Date: _____
Destination(s): _____
Weather: _____
First Impressions of the Area:

_____

Morning Adventures:

_____

Afternoon Discoveries:

_____

Evening Relaxation:

_____

A Local Dish I Tried:

- Name: _____
- Where: _____
- Cost: _____
- Rating: _____

Highlight of the Day:

_____
_____
_____
_____
_____
_____
_____

Day 2

Day: _____
Date: _____
Location(s) Visited: _____
Weather: _____

Morning Highlights:

_____
_____

Afternoon Adventures:

_____
_____

Evening Moments:

_____
_____

Local Flavors I Tried (Food/Drink):

- Dish/Drink: _____
- Where: _____
- Cost: _____
- Impressions: _____

Most Memorable Moment of the Day:

_____
_____

Notes/Thoughts Before Bed:

_____
_____
_____

Day 3

Day: _____
Date: _____
Location(s) Visited: _____
Weather: _____

Morning Highlights:

_____
_____

Afternoon Adventures:

_____
_____

Evening Moments:

_____
_____

Local Flavors I Tried (Food/Drink):

- Dish/Drink: _____
- Where: _____
- Cost: _____
- Impressions: _____

Most Memorable Moment of the Day:

_____
_____

Notes/Thoughts Before Bed:

_____
_____
_____

Made in United States
Troutdale, OR
02/28/2025